D0229940

H.R.H. Prince
Charles

by Anwar Hussein

Introduction by
Wynford Vaughan-Thomas

Hamlyn
London · New York · Sydney · Toronto

Contents

ACKNOWLEDGEMENTS
All colour and black and white photographs
are by Anwar Hussein except for those on the
following pages: Camera Press Limited 15,
17 bottom, 27, 31, 110, 113 top; Central Press
Photos Limited 12 top, 13, 14 bottom, 17 top,
62 bottom, 101 bottom, 103 top; Fox Photos
Limited 12 bottom, 14 top, 16, 19, 20, 21, 23,
36; Keystone Press Agency Limited 18, 22, 24,
28, 63, 64, 68; Popperfoto 82, 117;
Syndication International Limited 26, 32, 51,
52, 62 top, 109 bottom.

Published by
The Hamlyn Publishing Group Limited
London · New York · Sydney · Toronto
Astronaut House, Feltham, Middlesex,
England

Created, designed and produced by
Trewin Copplestone Publishing Limited,
London

ISBN 0 600 37203 0

© Trewin Copplestone Publishing Limited
1978
All rights reserved. No part of this publication
may be reproduced, stored in a retrieval
system, or transmitted, in any form or by any
means, electronic, mechanical, photocopying,
recording or otherwise, without the
permission of The Hamlyn Publishing
Group Limited and the copyright holder.

Phototypeset in Britain
by Keyfilm (Trendbourne Ltd)
Colour origination by Autographic
Printed in Italy

Introduction

It is now just thirty years since I stood, microphone in hand, outside Buckingham Palace on the evening of 14 November 1948, looking out over a huge and happy crowd chanting with cheerful determination, 'We want the King. We want the Queen. We want Prince Philip.' At last the royal party came out onto the balcony, and a great wave of cheering swept the thousands jammed to the very gates of the palace. I've seen and described many royal appearances on that famous balcony, but I knew that the cheering on this occasion had an unusual depth and warmth to it. The announcement had just been made that a son had been born to the Princess Elizabeth, and everyone in that vast crowd felt that this was a very special occasion. An heir to the throne had appeared. The succession of the monarchy was assured. Now Britain could face the hard task of post-war recovery with renewed vigour and confidence. Such was the mood of the crowd outside the palace on that November day.

Not everyone in Britain shared that feeling, but to the vast majority of the people of these islands the monarchy still represented something solid, unchanging and worthwhile. They could not conceive of a Britain without it. The long ordeal of the war seemed to have added new strength to the links between the King and his country.

Since then, there have been profound changes in Britain. Our world role has diminished. Within the country the emphasis has been placed increasingly on social equality. Voices have been raised questioning the validity of an institution like the monarchy as this troubled century enters its closing decades. No one doubts that our present Queen – with the Duke of Edinburgh at her side – has amply filled the role of a modern monarch. The people look to the Queen, above all, as an example of personal integrity and devotion to duty. They want her to uphold standards and values in her public and family life. These expectations Her Majesty has magnificently fulfilled.

But what of the future? Can the remarkable personal respect and loyalty that the Queen has built around herself during the twenty-five years of her reign be transferred to her successor, for more than ever before the personality of the monarch is vitally important. In the past the institution of monarchy was more important than the character of the king who occupied the throne. Indeed, there have been some curious occupants of that exalted position – George IV, for example, whose private conduct was extraordinary, to say the least. Yet he left untouched the respect that people felt for the institution he represented. Today a George IV is not possible. The monarchy retains its hold because of the examples set by the monarch. For all those who wish the institution to continue – and in truth this means the majority of the people of Britain – the character of the heir to the throne is of crucial importance. What sort of a man is Prince Charles?

For the first twenty years the Queen and the Duke very wisely tried to give him as normal a life as possible under the almost unbearable glare of publicity that inevitably surrounds the royal family. 'It's like living in a glass-house,' has been Charles's own description of it. The public read the usual gossipy pieces in the press about his career at Gordonstoun and at Cambridge, but they could not judge the real prince until he had started to play his part in public life. For me, the turning point came in 1969, the year of the investiture, when Prince Charles was twenty-one.

He had been created Prince of Wales some years before, for the title is not automatically inherited but is in the gift of the sovereign. Modern, youthful, Welsh-speaking Wales has been distinctly critical of the way holders of the title have regarded it in the past. The last Prince of Wales, Llywelyn ap Gruffydd, was killed in 1282 during the final Welsh War of Edward the First. The victorious king later conferred the title on his son, born in Caernarvon Castle. There is no evidence that throughout the mediaeval period the Princes of Wales felt any special affection for their principality. The Tudors, with their Welsh origin, were different, and the Stuarts, too, enjoyed Welsh loyalty. But the Hanoverians were totally indifferent. George IV did, indeed, pay one visit to his principality when he was Prince of Wales. He rode a few yards over the border from Shropshire, after a good lunch, to be greeted by the assembled gentry at the tree still proudly marked as the Prince's Oak, near Welshpool. He stayed for a few minutes and departed as swiftly as he had come. Lloyd George revived the investiture ceremony in 1911, but the late Duke of Windsor has left on record his feeling of embarrassment and discomfort at Caernarvon. How would Prince Charles react?

A few weeks before the ceremony he was invited to be the guest of honour at the annual eisteddfod of Urdd Gobaith Cymru (The Welsh League of Youth), a powerful Welsh youth movement in which the emphasis is strongly placed on the Welsh language. The audience expected no more than a few halting words in Welsh, followed by the usual apology for being 'unable to say more in your ancient and beautiful language.' Charles stepped forward and began not just a short sentence but a long speech in Welsh, beautifully pronounced and full of wit and sense. There was first a gasp of astonishment from the audience and then a huge roar of approval. Charles will not claim that he is fluent in Welsh, but he had spent a term at the University College of Aberystwyth in making certain he knew what he was saying and trying to understand the feeling in modern Wales. From that electrifying moment he became a true Prince of Wales. He has maintained his interest with constant visits to the principality and is an active chairman of the Prince of Wales' Committee for Safeguarding the National Environment. No wonder one of the Prince's entourage leaned over to me after that speech and remarked quietly, 'I think we are on a winner here.'

This feeling has now spread through the country. Prince Charles is very clear about the role he has to play and its importance for the future. He himself has said that he fully recognizes that, as people become more radical, there may be periods in the future when there is much less interest in having a monarchy, but he added, 'I maintain that the greatest function of any monarchy is the human concern which its representatives have for people, especially in what is becoming an increasingly inhuman era – an age of computers, machines, multi-national organizations. This, to my mind, is where the future can be promising.'

With Prince Charles as heir to the throne the future of royalty certainly looks promising. He is the one man who can safely carry the monarchy into the uncertain 21st century.

Wynford Vaughan-Thomas

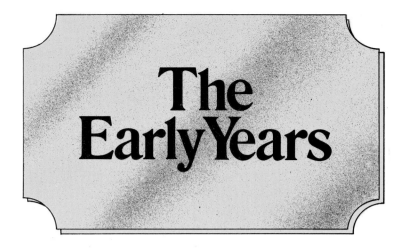

The Early Years

'HER ROYAL HIGHNESS, THE
PRINCESS ELIZABETH, DUCHESS OF
EDINBURGH, WAS SAFELY DELIVERED
OF A PRINCE AT 9.14 THIS EVENING,
NOVEMBER 14, 1948. HER ROYAL
HIGHNESS AND THE INFANT PRINCE
ARE BOTH WELL.'

With these words from the Home Secretary the world learned of the birth of Charles Philip Arthur George, a baby destined to the English throne.

Crowds had been gathering outside Buckingham Palace since early on that cold and rainy Sunday morning. They had heard that Sir William Gilliatt, the gynaecologist, was staying at the palace and, realizing that the birth of a new royal baby was imminent, enthusiastically awaited news.

When the time came, there was no need for the customary bulletin to be posted on the palace railings. A palace official whispered to a policeman who, in turn, passed on the news to the crowd. Immediately there broke out a spontaneous chorus of *For He's A Jolly Good Fellow* and by the time that Queen Mary drove up to see her first grandchild, celebrations were well under way.

It hadn't been a particularly easy birth. The Duke of Edinburgh, to help pass the time, had changed into flannels and a roll-neck sweater and was playing a frantic game of squash with his friend and equerry, Michael Parker, when he was told that he had become the father of a healthy baby boy weighing 7lb 6oz. He hurried upstairs to find his wife still under anaesthetic and eagerly took his first glimpse at his son. When Princess Elizabeth awoke from the anaesthetic, it was to the sight of her delighted husband holding a huge bouquet of roses and carnations.

The birth came at a time when the country was still feeling the aftermaths of war and the happy announcement cheered up everyone. Letters and presents poured in from all over the world and twelve temporary typists had to be employed to acknowledge the correspondence.

A child's green ration book for the use of Prince Charles was presented to the palace with the compliments of the Ministry of Food, thus giving a perfect example of the economic state of the country at that time.

Princess Elizabeth admires her first child

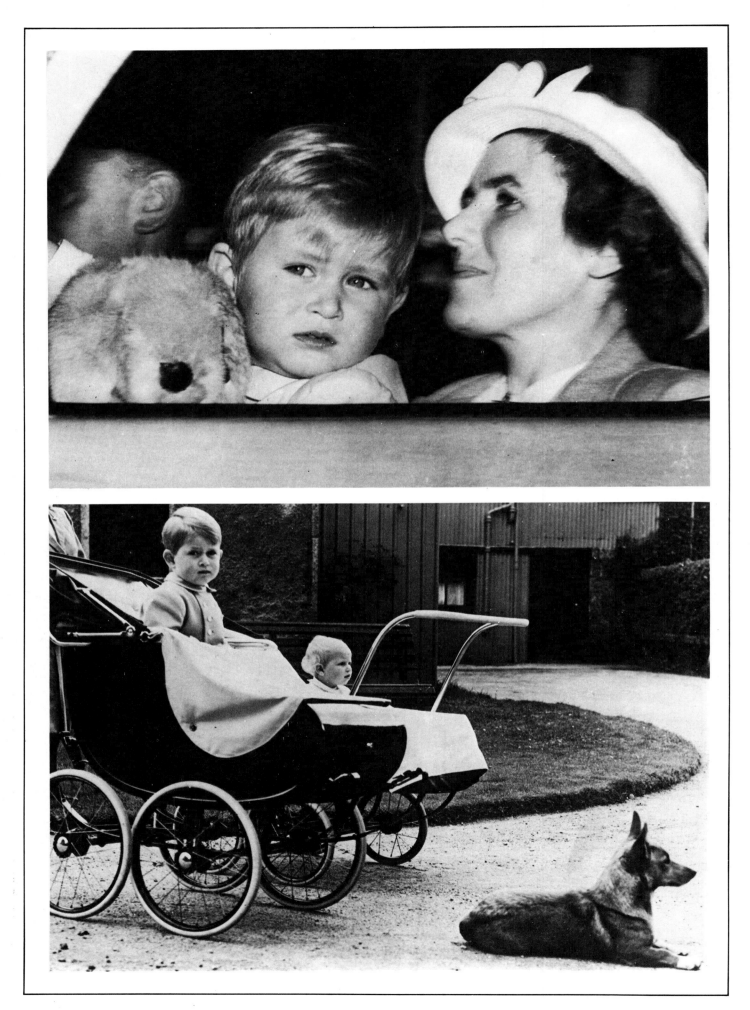

Two Scottish nurses were hired to look after the baby prince, Nurse Helen Lightbody, who had looked after the Duke of Gloucester's children, and Nurse Mabel Anderson, who had answered an advertisement in a nurses' magazine. Their empire was the pale blue nursery at Clarence House, into which Princess Elizabeth, husband and child moved in 1949 after conversions had been completed.

The long process of learning the attitudes, actions and activities that befitted a future king now began.

Prince Charles was christened in December 1948 in the Music Room at Buckingham Palace. Only relatives and close friends were present. The baby's grandfather, George VI, and the Duke of Edinburgh wore morning dress while Princess Elizabeth wore a long red coat and brown hat. The baby followed family tradition by being dressed in the christening robe of Honiton lace that the royal family have used for successive generations since Queen Victoria's second child, Edward, was christened in 1842. White narcissi, Christmas roses and white heather decorated the font, which had been brought over from the Gold Pantry at Windsor. The organist of the Chapel Royal played Handel's *Water Music* on the piano as the boys of the Chapel Royal choir filed into the room wearing their Tudor uniforms of scarlet and gold.

It was Princess Margaret who handed the baby to the Archbishop of Canterbury and announced in a clear voice the four names of her first nephew, 'Charles Philip Arthur George'.

Princess Elizabeth was determined to be with her children as much as possible. It wasn't always easy, but each morning she made a point that the little boy and his sister, Princess Anne, who was born almost two years later, were brought to see her from 9.00 to 9.30. Each evening the Princess and her husband would go to the nursery for an hour or so before she bathed her children and tucked them up in bed.

Prince Charles's only memory of his grandfather, George VI, was when the king attended his grandson's third birthday party. Sadly, he was to die soon after, in January 1952.

Opposite top: Prince Charles, aged two, holding a woolly toy, leaves Clarence House for an afternoon drive
Opposite bottom: Prince Charles, Princess Anne and a family pet on holiday in Scotland
Below: Prince Charles, Princess Anne and the Queen Mother watch the meet of the West Norfolk Hunt at Hillington

Right: Accompanied by their grandparents, the young Prince and Princess journey to Balmoral for a holiday

Opposite: Four-year-old Prince Charles, sporting long trousers, stands beside his father, Prince Philip, who is wearing the royal kilt

Below: Prince Charles on his third birthday with his grandfather, King George VI, his grandmother and his sister

The coronation of Queen Elizabeth II took place when the Prince was just four and a half years old. Looking very smart in a cream silk blouse and trousers, he was allowed to watch the service from the royal box at Westminster Abbey. 'Grannie, isn't it nice?' he whispered as he stood proudly between the Queen Mother and his aunt, Princess Margaret.

The new Queen wanted her children to be brought up as normally as possible, She realized that, as heir to the throne, the Prince was bound to be in the public eye, but she tried to make sure that the little boy and his sister would get less exposure than she and Princess Margaret had had as children.

She and Prince Philip rarely tried to restrict their children's playtime activities unless there was any actual danger, but Prince Philip insisted on basic disciplines, such as the young prince making his own bed and arriving punctually for meals. Servants were instructed to call the children by their first names when young, not 'Your Royal Highness', and there were the normal restrictions on pocket money and not always getting their own way.

As a small boy, Prince Charles seemed to be fairly unconcerned by any fuss. He was a sensitive child and responded quickly to harsh words and criticism. His sister Anne, on the other hand, was worried by few people. Whereas Charles never copied his mother's childhood caper of passing and repassing the palace guardsmen for the fun of seeing them salute, Princess Anne discovered the game very early in life.

When Charles was five years old, Miss Catherine Peebles, later to be known as Miss P or Mispy, arrived at the palace with the task of teaching the young prince reading, writing, arithmetic, geography, history and, later, French. In the past it had always been royal practice for the heir to the throne to be taught privately, but the question soon arose as to whether, in this modern democracy, it might not be better for the boy to have the opportunity of mixing with as wide a group of young people as possible.

His parents decided to break with tradition and, at the age of eight, Charles Philip Arthur George began school.

Above: During the Prince's visit to the dairy farm at Balmoral Castle a calf escapes from his grip

Opposite: Prince Charles, the Queen and Prince Philip arrive at the Royal Windsor Horse Show

Below: Prince Charles and Princess Anne reading in the Picture Gallery at Buckingham Palace

Schooldays and the Student Prince

Prince Charles began his schooldays at Hill House, a small private school in Knightsbridge. The school gave the young prince, who up to now had led a rather sheltered life, a chance to mix with youngsters his own age. It was here he played his first organized game of football, and his first report showed that he was very good at reading and loved history.

After two terms at Hill House, Charles was ready to go, as a boarder, to his father's old preparatory school, Cheam, on the Berkshire downs. Prince Philip had always gone to boarding schools and was very keen that his son should be given the same opportunities to prepare him for later life.

At first young Charles didn't appear too happy. Matters weren't helped by the press, which at one time harassed the school to such a degree that the editors of the London newspapers were called to Buckingham Palace and told by the Queen's press secretary that unless the school stopped being bothered, the Queen would have no alternative but to take Charles away and have him educated privately. Happily, Prince Charles soon made friends and settled down to the routine of school life, though he

Prince Charles boarding a bus with other pupils of Hill House School being taken to Chelsea for the school's sports day

Prince Charles looks very determined as he makes a run

later admitted that he found it pretty tough going at times. By the end of his first term he was summed up as 'still a little shy, but very popular; passionately keen on progressing at games; academically a good scholar.'

It was during his time at Cheam that Prince Charles was created Prince of Wales and Earl of Chester. The Queen had planned to make the announcement at the closing ceremony of the sixth British and Commonwealth Games in Cardiff Arms Park on 26 July 1958. Unfortunately, she was taken ill and her doctors advised her not to attend the ceremony. A recording of her speech was rushed to Cardiff, where it was introduced by Prince Philip. The speech ended with the words:

> I have therefore decided to mark it [this occasion] further by an act which will, I hope, give as much pleasure to all Welshmen as it does to me. I intend to create my son Charles Prince of Wales today. When he is grown up I will present him to you at Caernarvon.

The stadium erupted as the crowd roared with delight and burst into singing *God Bless the Prince of Wales*.

It was also at Cheam that Prince Charles caught chicken pox. Not long after that he was rushed to hospital to have his appendix removed.

At the age of thirteen it was time for Prince Charles to move on, and he entered the tough, physically testing world of Gordonstoun School in Scotland.

Charles's name had been put down for Eton at birth, but Prince Philip pressed for his old school, which he believed would help to give his son the self-confidence he needed. And so it was decided.

From the start no favours were extended to the Prince and he was treated as just one of the boys. It was a rigorous routine and the sport was extremely competitive, but Charles threw himself into the life and rugged outdoor activities with natural gusto.

The boys rose at 7.00 am and, whatever the weather, ran around the school grounds wearing nothing but gym shoes and shorts. This was followed by a cold bath. Lessons took place in the mornings and afternoons were spent in the open air, either on the playing fields, or on the various adventure courses, such as sailing or camping.

Prince Charles (facing camera) during the gun drill, which formed part of his school's field day

Charles was a popular boy at Gordonstoun and formed some solid friendships well outside the blue-blooded world from which he came. He was a great mimic and had tremendous fun impersonating masters and frightening the other boys if they were doing something wrong. His headmaster recalls:

The one thing that struck me about his sense of humour was that it was always kind. It might bite a bit here and there, but he never set out to upset or hurt anyone. He really enjoyed making people laugh and he was the first to laugh at himself if someone succeeded in getting his own back. He had his leg pulled often by the other boys and it never upset him. He was the first to come back with an answering quip.

The school aimed to give the boys a good all-round education and believed in developing the mind as well as the body. Music, classical reading and drama were encouraged. Academically, Charles was a pretty average student. His love of history remained, but he could never master mathematics. It soon became obvious that the youngster had an artistic streak and Charles felt himself drawn to the stage. His first chance to don greasepaint and face the footlights came when the school put on a full production of *Macbeth*, with Charles in the title role.

One of the many advantages of Gordonstoun was that it was so far away from Fleet Street. But the Prince learned the hard way that the world's press always took an obsessive interest in a future king. News got out that Charles, aged 14, had been seen drinking cherry brandy in a local pub. International news hounds descended en masse and within hours the world heard about Charles's fall from grace. It was a lesson he would never forget.

When the Prince reached the age of seventeen, his parents thought it was time for a change and, as usual, discussed the matter with their son. Prince Philip thought that a spell in Australia would do Charles the world of good. It would widen his horizons, toughen him up and keep him out of the limelight. The Queen thought it an excellent idea to put the heir to the throne in the lap of the Commonwealth – and so a three month exchange with a pupil from Geelong Gramar School was arranged.

Charles admitted he was slightly apprehensive about going to Australia. He had heard that 'Aussies' tended to give 'pommies' a hard time. But he needn't have worried. Almost as soon as he arrived the Prince felt completely at home:

Accompanied by schoolchums, the newly created Prince of Wales walks back to Cheam School after attending church

Prince Charles arriving for his first term at Gordonstoun, accompanied by his father, is greeted by the headmaster, Mr Robert Chew

I was concerned about how I would be received and how I would appear to them. But after I had been there an hour I realized that I had absolutely no need to worry. I found the people so friendly and welcoming.

He settled down quickly to his new environment and found Timbertop, the bush annexe of Geelong Grammar School, every bit as rigorous as Gordonstoun. The point of the Geelong educational system was to teach initiative and self-reliance. The boys had to do almost everything for themselves except cook their own meals. Every weekend they went on tough bush expeditions and each week they had to complete two cross-country runs. During a brief visit to Sydney on an official engagement Charles was asked by pressmen what he considered to be the most useful thing he had learned at the bush school. With a straight face the Prince replied,

Kangaroo wrestling. You creep up on your opponents from behind, grab them by the tail, flip them on their backs and then you have them at your mercy.

Prince Charles felt he really grew up in Australia and quite obviously adored his time there. And the

Above: the Prince takes to cycling during his undergraduate days at Cambridge

Opposite: A hungry student Prince caters for himself

Aussies loved having the 'pommie' in their homeland. The visit was an unprecedented success for both sides, and by the time he left to return to England Charles had developed a deep love for the country that remains to this day.

On his return to Gordonstoun to finish his schooling, Charles was made guardian of the school. He worked and played hard. To the delight of his father, he became the proud owner of a silver medal of the Duke of Edinburgh's Award Scheme, which he earned for initiative during an expedition in the Cairngorms and for his achievements in athletics, pottery and first-aid.

Charles had developed a great deal at Gordonstoun. From the impish Cheam schoolboy of earlier years, he emerged as a sturdy, mature, healthy youth. The school had shaped him for manhood, exposed his artistic, musical and dramatic talents, and had given him firm, genuine friendships. This bright, informative young man was now ready for the next stage in his education.

In October 1967 Prince Charles arrived at Trinity College, Cambridge to read archaeology and anthropology. He enjoyed university tremendously, and a great deal of the new society found his interest. He joined in debates at the Cambridge Union with enthusiasm, played polo, took to riding a bike in common with fellow undergraduates, and was the life and soul of many a party. And, of course, there was the Cambridge Dramatic Society!

For many years Charles had been a fanatical lover of the popular radio comedy programme 'The Goon Show', and Cambridge quickly nurtured him to appreciate sophisticated and subtle humour. The two major revues in which he appeared were very funny and genuinely brought down the house on several occasions. Both revues were written by fellow students in the old 'Footlights' tradition and confirmed the Prince as a talented actor and ad-libber.

In a revue called 'Revolution', the Prince appeared in fourteen of the forty sketches. It was an avant-garde piece of theatre and an enormous success. Right in the middle Charles broke into an impromptu 'Goons' sketch, literally having a conversation with himself using the voices of the 'Goons' characters Eccles and Bluebottle.

Both the press and the audience agreed that he was superb, so it wasn't surprising that the following year he was selected for the next revue 'And Quiet Flows the Don'. This proved to be an even more hilarious success. The Prince had been given a considerable script to learn and members of the press were among the audience at the dress rehearsal. Everything went well until, in the middle of a sketch mimicking a television weather reporter, the moment every actor dreads arrived – Prince Charles forgot his lines.

There was a deathly hush as all eyes turned on the young man, who turned to the wings and, laughing, said, 'What the hell comes next?' The whole house

Right: Prince Charles meets the Goons: Peter Sellers, Michael Bentine and Spike Milligan
Below: During rehearsals for a Cambridge revue

For once unrecognized, the Prince walks down a Cambridge Street

erupted with laughter and the Prince had turned a potentially embarrassing moment into triumph. 'It doesn't happen like this at the BBC,' he quipped. Next day the incident had caused headlines all over the world.

Life at Cambridge was not all play and Prince Charles never neglected his studies. After three years, he gained a second class Bachelor of Arts degree in history.

All in all, this was considered a very credible result, considering that, unlike his fellow graduates, the Prince had had numerous absences to carry out duties of state. He had even spent a term away from Cambridge at the University College of Wales in Aberystwyth, where he had gone principally to study the Welsh language prior to his investiture as Prince of Wales, which took place at Caernarvon Castle in June 1969.

Although Prince Charles spent a happy three years at Trinity, there must have been times when life proved frustrating. Not all university life could be included in his personal curriculum. For example, political societies were closed to him, for the heir to the English throne must not appear to be political and is unable to make political statements or, indeed, any statement capable of political interpretation. This can't have been easy for an intelligent and well-informed young man intent on understanding the world. But Prince Charles had learned the necessity of steering clear of any controversies. By the time he left Cambridge he had established himself as a keen wit with an enormous sense of fun, popular among people of all ages and from all types of background.

While he was still an undergraduate, Prince Charles's plans for a career in the Royal Navy were announced. 'I am looking forward to it very much. I hope I shall not be too seasick,' he said.

The armed forces of Her Majesty's government were the natural continuation for the heir to the throne. Not only would he be following in his father's footsteps by joining the Royal Navy, but it was a very good way of learning how to govern other men. A ship is rather like a mini-kingdom, with the captain as monarch. Power is taught on a man-to-man level and leadership qualities come to the fore.

Before, Charles had always been the Prince of Wales first and friend and student after, but at sea he would be a seaman first and a 'royal' second.

His parents felt it was important for their son to have an all-round experience of military life, so before joining the navy, Charles was accepted as a graduate at the Royal Air Force College at Cranwell. He had already qualified for a private pilot's licence at the age of twenty-one, and in a BBC interview he recalled the first time he went solo in a plane.

I always thought I was going to be terrified. I was dreading the moment throughout training when I would have to go up alone. But on the day I went solo, the instructor taxied up to the end of the runway and suddenly climbed out and said, "You're on your own, mate!" So there I was and I hardly had time to get butterflies in my tummy before taking off. I was wondering whether I could do it, but the moment I was in the air it was absolutely marvellous. There was no instructor to breathe down my neck and the aeroplane flew much better because he had gone and the weight was not there. I had a wonderful time. Fortunately, I landed well the first time. That had been the only thing worrying me during the flight. I had visions of my going around and around until eventually the fuel ran out. But all was well.

At Cranwell the Prince flew 400 mph jets, phantom bombers and the new Nimrod anti-submarine jets as co-pilot, and emerged from the college a fully qualified pilot. He had also received notoriety by becoming the first heir-apparent to make a parachute jump. Charles's feet got tangled in the cords of his 'chute and he spent the first few seconds of his fall upside down, but he made a smooth landing into the English Channel.

The Prince of Wales gained his wings in mid-August 1971 and by mid-September he had entered

Lieutenant the Prince of Wales in his cabin on board HMS 'Bronington'

the Royal Naval College, Dartmouth to start his naval training and prepare for life at sea. Thirteen weeks later he was ready.

Charles was given a wide range of experience at sea and trained in seamanship, navigation, submarine escape techniques, naval communications and bridge watch-keeping. From the start Charles loved the navy and, with his all-pervading sense of humour well to the fore, he was quick to learn. He was the first to admit, however, that some aspects of military training suited him better than others. The non-mathematical prince was slightly dazed by the amount of computerized machinery he had to deal with and navigation did not prove to be his strong point. He told a reporter at the beginning of 1975,

The difficulty is that I did a shortened course of introduction to the navy, and a fairly short period of training. I have to try that little bit harder to assimilate all the vast amount of technical information and the navigational problems rather more quickly than other people had to do. The trouble is that people expect one to be a genius, at least, if nothing else.

By mid-1974, having been promoted to the rank of Acting Lieutenant, Charles was due to undergo a three month course of helicopter training at Yeovilton, Somerset. He succeeded brilliantly at Yeovilton and was awarded the double diamond trophy for the student who had made the most progress. Later, at an interview with the news editor of the *Evening Standard*, he admitted that this course was the aspect of his naval career which he enjoyed most.

I adore flying, and I personally can't think of a better combination than naval flying – being at sea and being able to fly. . . . I think that people that fly in the Fleet Air Arm are of a very high standard, particularly those chaps who fly Buccaneers and Phantoms. These people

are taking all kinds of risks. Taking off and landing on carriers, particularly at night, is no joke at all. If you're living dangerously, it tends to make you appreciate life that much more, and to really want to live it to its fullest. They're some of the most invigorating and amusing people that I've come across.

At Yeovilton the Prince completed 105 flying hours in 45 days, which is no mean achievement by any standard. His instructor, Lieutenant Commander Alan MacGregor, said that he was a model pupil and a natural pilot.

He has a natural aptitude for flying and genuinely loves it. Several times when he was flying solo I saw him get out of what might have been dangerous situations. Once, one of the helicopter's two engines caught fire. I saw the flames shooting up close beside him and knew there wasn't much time to spare. As I followed him down I watched him make a

Above: Learning to fly at Yeovilton

Opposite: Flying a Royal Navy helicopter

faultless emergency landing in a field. All the time he remained cool and collected, as though it were just another routine practice exercise.

Charles also underwent commando support training at the Royal Marines Training Centre at Lympstone in Devon. He took the tough course in his stride, but described the endurance and 'Tarzan' course as 'a most horrifying expedition'. He had to swing over small chasms on ropes, slide down the ropes at death-defying speeds and then walk across wires and climb up rope ladders strung between a pool and a tree.

The Prince made it clear that he wanted to join an operational helicopter squadron as soon as possible and, much to his amazement, the Admiralty agreed to let him fly in a front-line squadron.

He served as a naval pilot on the commando carrier HMS *Hermes*. It was on the *Hermes* that he visited the Arctic in April 1975, where he was invited to inspect the Undersea Research Centre and watch a demonstration of walking upside down on a fathom of ice under the sea. Having watched, fascinated, the Prince couldn't resist giving it a try. The temperature of the water was 28.5 degrees Fahrenheit and Charles described the whole affair in the magazine of the British Sub-Aqua Club, *Triton*.

I lowered myself gingerly through six foot of ice into the freezing water, already covered with newly-formed pieces of ice rather like a creme de menthe frappe. The result of my upside-down walk was highly comical in the extreme. I only partly succeeded. What was fascinating was to see the exhaust bubbles trapped on the underside of the ice and spread out like great pools of shimmering mercury.

Right: Prince Charles in flying gear
Below: As a qualified navy pilot, Charles is enormously proud of his 'Happy Hermes' T-shirt

Top: Charles in full naval uniform in Nepal with Earl Mountbatten of Burma

Above: The Prince at work and in command

As a commando pilot, life was pretty tough aboard the *Hermes*. It wasn't unusual to be up at six, facing the prospect of several lengthy flights, but between spells of work he led a normal officer's life, working in his cabin and often watching films after dinner. Keeping fit was also an important part of the routine – deck hockey and PT were both favoured pursuits.

Then, in February 1976 the Prince of Wales took over his first naval command, a minesweeper, HMS *Bronington*. The ship has a crew of five officers and thirty-four men and is known in the fleet as 'Old

Quarter Past Eleven' because of her pennant number, 1115.

Charles had an active command, and proved himself a natural leader and popular among his crew. He left the navy having achieved a considerable amount and having visited much of the world. But this was not all, for the navy had given Prince Charles a profession and, perhaps most important of all, 'It has given me a marvellous opportunity to get as close to the "ordinary" British chap as possible.'

The Investiture

Prince Charles has participated in many colourful ceremonies in his time, but undoubtedly the most splendid was his investiture as Prince of Wales, which took place at Caernarvon Castle on 1 July 1969.

Charles is the twenty-first Prince of Wales. The ancient ceremony dates back over six centuries to the time when Edward I had had to fight many battles against the Welsh princes before he could get them to accept him as their king. While he was in Wales, Edward had a son, born at Caernarvon Castle, and calling together all the chief Welshmen, he told them that he would give them the baby as their prince. And so the little boy, later Edward II, became the very first Prince of Wales.

Charles's investiture, at an estimated cost of a quarter of a million pounds, was watched on television by millions of people throughout the world. Despite the fact that an Opinion Research Centre poll showed that over half the young adults in Wales thought that the investiture was a waste of money, the whole episode proved a resounding success. Much of that success must have been due to the Prince himself. His obvious sincerity and his good humour in the face of insults won him a certain grudging respect from even the dourest opponents. The Mayor of Caernarvon, who had begun as a sceptic, called him 'the ace in the royal pack.'

The most serious threat came from militant Welsh nationalists. In the three months preceding the investiture seven bombs had been exploded in protest. The threats of violence were sustained to the end. The royal train, taking the Queen and her family to Caernarvon, had to make an unscheduled stop at Crewe after the discovery of a dummy bomb. An egg was thrown at the carriage in which the Queen, Prince Philip and Princess Anne were riding to the Castle, and there was an explosion in a railway siding just before the ceremony started.

Understandably, a massive security programme was launched. The Queen must have been seriously concerned, though she showed no signs of this in public. Prince Charles also hid his nerves extremely well, but admitted he was looking forward to the ordeal with mixed feelings. 'It will be an exhausting day and an enjoyable one, because I do enjoy ceremonies.' On the morning of the investiture he caught sight of himself on television and remarked cheerfully, 'It's always me – I'm getting rather bored with my face.'

The Prince had spent the term immediately prior to the investiture at the University College of Wales, Aberystwyth, where a programme of Welsh language studies had been mapped out for him. He was determined to show he was serious about Welsh, even though it is a fiendishly difficult language. After just two months at Aberystwyth, Charles's linguistic efforts were tested before the Welsh League of Youth, who were among the strongest critics of the investiture. He won them over completely and received a standing ovation, and it was generally agreed that his accent and mastery of the language were remarkably good. 'Having spent so many hours in the language laboratories here, I shall certainly never let it die without stout resistance,' the Prince told his delighted audience.

This was an encouraging curtain raiser to the investiture, when the Queen would present her son to the people of Wales and he would again have to make a speech in Welsh, this time with an audience of millions.

In the end, the investiture ceremony passed off remarkably smoothly. The worst moment for Charles must have been when he discovered he was sitting on his speech and had to wiggle the notes from under him in full view of the television cameras.

Opposite: Prince Charles kneels before his monarch as she places the coronet of the Prince of Wales on his head

Above: Watched by proud members of the royal family, the Prince, accompanied by his mother and father, leaves the dias to be presented to the people of his principality

Opposite: After the ceremony, the Queen and the Prince of Wales leave Caernarvon Castle, flanked by policemen and Beefeaters

The pomp and pageantry of the occasion impressed everyone. The simple but effective setting was designed by a team led by Lord Snowden, who had been the Castle's Constable since 1963. The Queen was greeted with the national anthems of Wales and England and the Garter King of Arms fetched the Prince from the room where he had been waiting. Bare-headed and wearing the uniform of Colonel-in-Chief of the Royal Regiment of Wales, Charles bowed three times and knelt before his monarch. The Queen then invested her son with his Sword of State, his golden sceptre, the princely mantle and the ring that symbolized his marriage to his country. Then, in one of the most moving moments in the whole ceremony, she placed the gold coronet of the Prince of Wales on his head and straightened the purple cloak around his shoulders. Placing his hands between hers, the Prince pledged his loyalty with the words:

I, Charles, Prince of Wales, do become your liege man of life and limb and of earthly worship, and faith and truth I will bear unto you to live and die against all manner of folks.

The two exchanged the kiss of fealty and Sir Bowen Thomas, president of the Prince's alma mater at Aberystwyth, read a loyal address from the people of Wales.

It was now time for the Prince of Wales to reply. Speaking to his people in their own language, he declared his firm intention to associate in word and deed with as much of the life of the principality as possible.

The demands on a Prince of Wales have altered, but I am determined to serve and to try as best I can to live up to those demands whatever they might be in the rather uncertain future.

One thing I am clear about, and it is that Wales needs to look forward without forsaking the traditions and essential aspects of her past. The past can be just as much a stimulus to the future as anything else. By the affirmation of your loyalty today, for which I express my gratitude, this will not simply be a faint hope.

At the end of the ceremony the Queen led her son to the battlements of Caernarvon Castle and, raising his hand, presented him to the people of his principality. And seeing the Prince resplendent in his investiture robes, it wasn't only the people of Wales who had tears in their eyes. . . .

The Sporting Prince

By far the most publicized of Prince Charles's sporting activities is the fast and exciting game of polo.

I love the game, I love the ponies, I love the exercise. It's also the one team game I can play. It's also a very convenient game for me as long as I spend my weekends at Windsor. It isn't convenient to play football; you can't just nip out of Windsor Castle and enjoy a soccer game. But if I knew that there was immense criticism of my playing polo, I'd have to think about it. You can't have everything you want, even if you feel it does no harm. People's susceptibilities count.

Polo is the perfect pastime for someone who loves horsemanship and the thrill of competitive sport, and Charles inherited his enthusiasm for the game from his father. Polo has always been one of Prince Philip's favourite sports, but he had to give it up in 1971 because of a damaged wrist. However, he enjoys watching his son play and can be happy in the knowledge that Charles is rapidly becoming one of the best players in the country.

There are some experts who point out that Charles cares too much for his horses to be as good a player as the Duke of Edinburgh, but his coach, Australian Sinclair Hill, reckons that he has more natural ability than his father. 'He is fearless, has great positional strength and a technique that's almost without fault.'

Charles made his debut in 1969, when he surprised experts by scoring a goal in his very first match. Since then he has gone from strength to strength, and in 1977 rose to the rank of international sportsman when he was chosen to play for Young England against France – his father played for England against Argentina in the mid-1960s.

Charles always seems happy and relaxed on a polo ground. Between games he spends a lot of time with his ponies, stroking their ears and offering them lumps of sugar, thus clearly demonstrating the close relationship between polo player and pony.

But the Prince's horsemanship is not only confined to the polo field. He also enjoys hunting and occasionally participates in cross-country events, where his wit helps him make the best of bad situations. 'That was excellent practice for parachuting,' he cheerily observed after having been thrown twice on a particularly rough course.

Although he survives these little mishaps with his usual good humour, he has every sympathy with his sister, Princess Anne, whose performance in international competitions is often disturbed by overeager photographers. Princess Anne is an accomplished horsewoman. She won the Individual European Three-Day Event at Burghley in 1971 and was the first member of the royal family to hold a European equestrian title. Her greatest triumph was

Left: Relaxing between chukkas
Opposite: All smiles as Charles's team wins

Opposite: Prince Charles with his favourite polo pony, Pam's Folly

Above: Perhaps Charles had a word with the pony before the polo match

**Above: Prince Charles is a very
proficient shot
Left: Thirsty work, polo – and the
Prince reckons he's earned this
refreshing mug of beer**

to be chosen for the British team in the 1976 Olympic Games, which took place in Montreal.

'From my sister's point of view,' says Charles, 'the behaviour of the photographers is very hard to take, and I can understand why. If you are doing something competitive in public, especially in the top international class, you are inevitably keyed up. To have a lot of people with cameras pursuing you, and possibly frightening the horse, is annoying, to say the least. It is easy to become irritable and to feel that it is only when things go wrong – when you are upside down or halfway up a tree – that photographs appear in the paper or on TV.'

There are plenty of other activities to keep Charles busy during his leisure hours. He is a proficient shot, swimmer, winter sportsman and fisherman, and seems willing to have a go at just about everything, however dangerous. 'But he's not a show-off,' says his uncle, Earl Louis Mountbatten of Burma. 'He is more fearless than anyone I have met and he does it because he enjoys trying things out for himself.'

The Prince has admitted that there is one sport that he would not like to try – rock climbing. 'I don't particularly like the idea of having to cling to a rock face by my fingernails.'

Without doubt, much of Charles's spirit of adventure was aroused at Gordonstoun, but a lot of inspiration must have come from his father, who has gained so much pleasure himself from physical exertion that he doesn't want others to miss out. Both father and son are excellent shots – among the best in the country – and many a happy day has been spent on the family estates at Sandringham and Balmoral. In fact, Charles first started grouse shooting at the age of ten, and three years later could be counted on for a decent bag of pheasants.

Charles is considered to be the best fisherman in the family and, like his grandmother, gets enormous pleasure from a quiet day's fishing.

It's interesting to note that most of Charles's outdoor pursuits are ones in which he has to rely on himself rather than be part of a team. He really is a bit of a loner. Even polo, though one is part of a team, is essentially a sport for individuals. Even at school he seemed to be more at home in individualistic sports rather than in team-games. At his prep school he did show enthusiasm for football and was even made captain of the school's First Eleven, but perhaps it is significant that during that season Cheam did not win one match. At Gordonstoun he made the rugby team, but all he earned was a broken nose.

Charles first started skiing in 1963. Having completed his first term at Gordonstoun, he spent part of the Christmas holidays in Switzerland with a group of German relatives 4000 feet up in the mountains in the resort of Tarasp. Unfortunately, hoards of relentless pressmen arrived on the scene, all eager to see the young prince make his first attempts on skis and Charles spent most of his time trying to dodge them. But he did manage to get in some sport and, in the end, got a medal for 'trying'. He also managed to get his own back on the press. As photographers waited, shutters at the ready, to catch the

Winning a cup is quite something, especially when it's filled with champagne. But by the look on Charles's face, he'd prefer that beer

43

Charles, like his grandmother, loves fishing. It seems to suit the contemplative side of his nature

Prince as he took a sleigh ride, Charles appeared brandishing his own camera and proceeded coolly and repeatedly to take pictures of the press.

On his return to Scotland he continued to practise his skiing technique. By the time the snows had melted he was proficient enough to be quite capable of speeding down even the most difficult slopes.

The sea has always given Charles a great deal of satisfaction. Of course, it was a constant presence at Gordonstoun and the Prince thoroughly enjoyed swimming and surf-riding, and gained a certificate for life-saving.

One of the benefits of being a royal child was that he enjoyed tuition from experts. It was Uffa Fox who taught him to sail, and in his first attempt at competitive sailing he beat his father in a Cowes Week race.

While he was in the navy, Charles got the opportunity to develop his enthusiasm for diving. During a trip to the West Indies he became particularly fond of diving for treasure near the wreck of a seventeenth century Spanish galleon. 'I can well imagine the disease which grips divers and dedicates them to their hobby or profession,' he commented.

He also explored a wreck off the British Virgin Islands and described swimming inside the hull of the sunken schooner 'as if it was some vast green cathedral filled with shoals of silver fish.'

Physically, Prince Charles is today an extremely fit man. He likes to keep in good condition and, like everyone, doesn't like the idea of getting older. He is already concerned about the slight thinning on top. When a photographer once drew attention to this fact in his newspaper, Charles sought him out next day and said, 'What do you mean – bald?'

But in no way is Charles slowing up. He rises early and either goes jogging or exercises rigorously, and certainly isn't the type to just sit around doing nothing. He takes pains to fill every spare moment with activity. In fact, he is very much like the Duke of Edinburgh in this respect.

Of course, there are other, less vigorous interests, which take up a lot of the Prince's spare time, He is heavily involved with youth work and is seriously concerned about how young people spend their leisure hours.

Prince Charles likes to have a go at everything. At a game fair in Wales he tries his hand at archery and boating (opposite)

I often feel that in urban areas there is a distinct lack of facilities for younger people and I feel sometimes that the kind of attitude you see – particularly, for instance, at football matches – is really that they are trying to get rid of pent-up energy and enthusiasm, and to my mind it seems misdirected.

'I just feel that they could be given opportunities – not just going to a football match, but other things – where they can get rid of their energy.

During the Queen's Silver Jubilee year Charles devoted himself to raising money for the Silver Jubilee Trust, the aim of which is to help young people help others. As a guide, the ideas should be based on the theme of action and adventure, like the mountain rescue, coastguard and surf life-saving work he did at Gordonstoun. The appeal received a tremendous response and young people are being encouraged to come up with ideas that will enable them to take part in useful, helpful activities in the community in which they live.

And though Prince Charles is older than the seven-to-twenty-five age group with which he is concerned, he is certainly in harmony with modern youth and their problems. When he opened a large sports complex in Watford, having looked at the swimming pools and the tennis and squash courts, he asked, 'Where are the skateboard parks? Isn't that the way to keep youngsters off the streets and prevent them breaking their necks among traffic?'

Anthropology is another subject close to the Prince's heart and he is patron of the Royal Anthropological Institute. He took part in a BBC series 'Face Values', which compared ideas in five countries and in Britain and showed the difference of describing others in terms of our own culture.

Charles admitted that the series was the result of a statement he had made at a dinner given by the Royal Anthropological Institute:

With supreme disregard for the dictates of caution and diplomacy, I urged that a great deal of good could be achieved by well-made films, primarily in order to explain to people living in this country the reasons for our behaviour and to show the similarities that exist even in the apparent differences between ourselves and other races. My belief rested on the feeling that if only more people could have the advantage of information and knowledge about other people's social behaviour, customs, religion and so forth, then perhaps some of the prejudice against immigrant groups in this country might be slowly reduced.

When he gets the chance, Charles also enjoys watching television, but tries to stick to watching selected programmes, such as good documentaries and comedy shows like 'Monty Python' and 'The Goodies'. 'I find television a great drug and before you know where you are, you just sit there with your eyes becoming square.'

To suit the contemplative side of his nature, Prince Charles likes to play the cello, but finds he has very little time nowadays to keep it up.

I like music very much. I liked playing it – I haven't so much time now – and I like listening to it. The trouble is that if you don't practise, you simply can't enjoy your own noise. It was the rich, deep sound of the cello that first appealed to me.

Charles enjoys jazz and pop music, particularly the Beatles, but tends to prefer classical music.

Rhythm is very important to him and when he hears rhythmic music, he just wants to get up and dance. His private rooms at Buckingham Palace are filled with expensive hi-fi and recording equipment. He also loves opera and is president of the Friends of Covent Garden.

When it comes to reading, Charles admits that he sometimes finds it difficult to keep awake for long once he has sat down with a book.

> But I do love reading very much and used to do a lot of it when I was at sea and had more time. I tend to read a lot of history and a lot of biographies. I'm also fascinated by some of the books by Alexander Solzhenitsyn.

A subject that the Prince never tires of is archaeology. He first became interested in it at Gordonstoun and went on to study it at Cambridge. His

Charles successfully negotiates a water-jump during a hunter trials

numerous trips overseas give him plenty of opportunity to keep his interest alive.

Charles also tries his hand at painting watercolours, but finds it 'frightfully difficult'.

One sport – if you can call it a sport – that he finds quite as enjoyable as skiing or playing polo is flying. He qualified for a private pilot's licence at the age of twenty-one and has since clocked up a considerable number of flying hours. He is also a skilled helicopter pilot, qualified in air-sea rescue.

'I tend to be a jack-of-all trades,' says Charles, but there are many people who would dispute this. After all, could a jack-of-all-trades pilot a jet, or represent England at polo, or land a helicopter in a cabbage patch?

Right: Just a quiet word between friends

Opposite: Dressed for a day in the country, walking stick in hand

The Prince on Tour

W hy, he isn't snobbish at all,' declared an amazed Canadian lady during one of Charles's visits to her country. And indeed the Prince has gained the reputation of endearing himself to everyone he meets. It's actually getting the chance to talk to people that presents a problem.

In a sense, one is alone, and the older I get, the more alone I become,' explains Charles. 'Unfortunately, the nicest people are those who won't come up and make themselves known. They're terrified of being seen to be friendly in case they'll be accused of sucking up to me and because they imagine, quite wrongly, that I won't want to talk to them. When I was much younger and did not really understand this, I used to think: Good God, what's wrong? Do I smell? Have I changed my shoes?

I realize now that I have to make a bit of the running and show that I am a reasonable human being. An awful lot of people say eventually, "Good Lord, you're not nearly as pompous as I thought you were going to be." So one has, in that sense, a lonely existence, but I've got perfectly used to it. It just requires a bit more effort.

Opposite: Prince Charles in Ghana

Above: Wearing garlands presented to him, Prince Charles meets dancers in Fiji

Above: An amusing moment as the Prince meets the winner of Canada's national Indian princess contest

Opposite: Charles, bedecked in flowers, receives a warm welcome in Papua New Guinea

Since his investiture in 1969, Charles had made more and more personal appearances on tours throughout the world. He went on his first solo royal tour in 1970 just after leaving university, when he represented the Queen at the independence celebrations in Fiji, and afterwards visited the Gilbert and Ellice Islands. He requested that his activities be as informal as possible. 'The whole idea of these visits,' he explained, 'is for me to meet as many people as I can so they can see for themselves I'm a pretty ordinary sort of person and not different to anyone else.'

On joining the navy, Charles realized he would probably get plenty of opportunity to go overseas.

I hope that if I do go abroad I could combine it with visiting various places and being a kind of ambassador.

In fact, this proved to be the case and during his navy years Charles went on several 'goodwill' visits

around the globe. Of course, there were problems. As soon as the Prince joined his first ship in Gibraltar the stresses and intrigues of international politics appeared. The Spanish government was not at all pleased at the presence of a British prince on the Rock, which had been a point of contention between the Spanish and British governments for some time. Only two weeks later it was rumoured that Charles's ship, HMS *Norfolk*, was staying clear of Malta because British relations with Malta's prime minister, Dom Mintoff, were not running smoothly at the time. In fact, the rumour was without foundation, and Charles did go to Malta and even spent a day water-skiing with Prime Minister Mintoff. Over the next few years immense tact had to be used in planning the ports of call for the Prince's ship, and visits to countries considered controversial were cancelled.

It was while he was attached to HMS *Hermes* that Charles visited Canada in 1975, a royal trip that was

hailed by the Canadian press as 'the warmest ever'. The Prince spent the first three days at the Canadian capital, Ottawa. The Canadian press talked of 'Charlie mania', which indicates how popular the heir to the thrown had become across the Atlantic. The British press were equally enthusiastic and suggested that Charles had charmed enough people to be registered as a valuable national resource.

Charles told secondary school pupils attending a 'model heads of Commonwealth' meeting that 'the most important thing a person in my position could have is a sense of humour . . . being able to laugh at oneself.' He said that he was an ordinary person, that he liked people to tell him so, and that he found his job 'fascinating'.

On being asked what was to be his future role as King of Canada, the Prince answered, 'I might not be king for forty years, so I don't know what my role will be.' He added that he has to be very careful when speaking to a girl, because she 'immediately gets sized up as my future spouse.'

The second part of the Canadian trip caused the most sensation. In complete contrast to the various engagements in Ottawa, Charles flew up to the frozen Northwest Territories to participate in some entirely new activities. He was determined to sample as much as he could of life in the land of the Eskimo.

Almost the first thing he did when he stepped out of his plane on a remote airfield was to go for a ride on an Eskimo sledge pulled by a team of huskies. Soon getting bored with just being a passenger, he took over driving the team himself and, on his return quipped, 'That just sleighed me.' Charles's wit was very much in evidence throughout the tour and the Eskimos loved him for it. He enjoyed many more snowmobile and dogsled rides. During one ride, which lasted four hours, he stopped off for a polar picnic of musk-ox stew. Dressed from head to toe in caribou fur, he joked, 'I hope we don't meet a polar bear because he might think I'm in season.'

During his visit to the territories Charles saw the lighting of a gas flare at a natural gas well, lunched with bush pilots, and flew to the majestic Arctic landscape of Grise Fiord in the extreme north. Here he visited a community of one hundred Eskimos. Eskimo life fascinated him and he insisted on going inside an igloo to see for himself how his future subjects lived. The Eskimos showed him how they built their igloos and how some of them could be made in as little as fifteen minutes, a perfect protection against sudden storms. The Prince also watched the Eskimos fishing through the ice for seals and, to his horror, was soon offered the local delicacy – raw seal meat!

Prince Charles, swathed in furs to beat the cold, visited Canada's Northwest Territories in April 1975

Charles later described the incident:

> For the honour of the family I picked up a piece of meat and made the fatal error, of course, of chewing it rather than swallowing it like a sheep's eye. The trouble is that it tasted absolutely appalling. I said, "The Press here are going to eat this and all the people with me . . .,you'll all eat it." They shrank away and disappeared. A doctor who was with us muttered in their ears that they shouldn't eat it because it was probably a week old. So I said "Thank you very much, chummy, what about me, eh?!"

The highlight of the visit to Canada's far north was at Resolute Bay, where for half an hour Charles dived below the five-foot thick Arctic ice, wearing a special rubber suit with hot air circulating inside. As the press and a group of puzzled Eskimos huddled around a tent that protected the hole through which Charles had disappeared into the freezing waters, the future king leapt out, his diving suit monstrously swollen with the compressed air used to insulate him from the cold, wearing a soggy bowler hat that he had retrieved from the seabed fifty feet down. The bowler had been planted there for the Prince to find, but Charles was less amused – 'very upset' in fact – also to find an empty beer can and two 45-gallon oil drums.

He had made the descent accompanied by Dr Joe MacInnes, the first man to swim below the North Pole, and Richard Mason, another diver, who had established the four-foot-square hole for scientific underwater research. The entire exercise was extremely hazardous. 'The water is so darned cold that in an ordinary diver's wet suit he would be dead in three minutes,' mentioned one official, but Charles had expressed a great interest in the under-the-ice experiments and was determined to see for himself what was going on. It was such an unlikely situation that even the security men were taking pictures!

At dinner that night the Prince won a standing ovation by performing in a sing-song concert. He launched a vocal reprisal, in harmony with members of his household, against the press corps, who had offered choruses about the problems of covering his procession through the Arctic. Forewarned, he had penned a little piece to the tune of the hymn *Immortal, Invisible, God Only Wise*. One of the four verses ran:

> Disgraceful, most dangerous to share the same plane,
> Denies me the chance to scratch and complain.
> Oh, where, may I ask, is the monarchy going,
> When princes and pressmen are in the same Boeing?

The older Prince Charles gets, the better his relationship with the press seems to be. He must find it frustrating when newspapers sensationalize his romantic and sporting activities and then steer clear of the very hard work that his position entails. But he remains philosophical about it.

> When I was younger, I sometimes used to get cross. Then, as I got older, I tried to think it out. I knew I mustn't go on being cross or shouting at people – it wasn't becoming in one so young. So I tried to understand the other person's position and put myself in his shoes. Part of that means recognizing the demands a

Rubber-suited, the Prince prepares to dive beneath the Arctic ice

newspaper makes of all the people who work on it, even if they own it. Anyway, it's when nobody wants to write about you or take a photograph of you that you ought to worry in my sort of job. Then there would be no point in being around – and I couldn't stand being around if there didn't seem to be any point to it.

The press, in their turn, have developed a sound respect for the Prince and especially appreciate his humour.

The Queen's Silver Jubilee year was rife with speculations about Charles's romances. On his way to an official tour of Ghana and the Ivory Coast, the Prince decided to spend a few days on a private visit to Kenya. While he was on a wildlife safari, rumours started that a mysterious, glamorous blonde was sharing his romantic Kenyan adventure. As he watched a bevy of beautiful flamingoes flutter past him on Kenya's Lake Nakuru, Charles laughed at photographers, 'You have caught me with plenty of birds this time – isn't it a pity they are only the feathered variety?' He was greatly amused by stories about the mystery blonde who had supposedly been spotted at his camp. 'If you read the British newspapers, the bush was thick with the other kind of birds when I was on safari,' he joked.

When he arrived at Nairobi airport to continue his journey, Charles went up to a group of waiting newsmen, and said, 'I think this is what you have been looking for,' and handed them a mysterious parcel. It turned out to be a bird, a stuffed pigeon, which had some blonde human hair glued to its head. A note enclosed in the parcel said, 'I've heard about this mysterious blonde. There you are then – a mysterious bird.' Everybody around erupted with laughter, but Charles left Kenya leaving one intriguing mystery for the press – where did he get the hair?

Prince Charles has travelled far and wide across the world, but it is the Commonwealth countries that are his regular hosts, and preserving the Commonwealth is one of Charles's great aims in life.

The whole question fascinates me. There is an enormous amount to be done there; it's one of those associations which require a great deal of effort and expertise to make it work satisfactorily and usefully in world terms.

Charles is a passionate believer in racial equality and he firmly believes that the Commonwealth, with its common language, culture and experience, can help break down the differences between people and give them a feeling of belonging.

I think there must be something unique about the Commonwealth, in that it has remained in being as long as it has. There must be some deep bond that's worth developing.

He realizes that the Queen, as head of the Commonwealth, plays an important part in keeping it together, but Charles pins his hopes for the future on the young people in member countries.

Above all, I believe it is up to the young of the Commonwealth to show that they believe that association has something to offer the modern world, because without your support, interest and encouragement, it will only be a matter of time before the whole thing fades away through lack of interest,

he told a gathering of two hundred young Commonwealth delegates.

Any organization that can contribute towards the destruction of artificial barriers between people of different races, creeds and cultures always gains the interest of the Prince. He has recently become president of the International Council of United World Colleges, and looks upon this position as an opportunity to meet people from every country and actually get things done for them. The United World Colleges is a group of private schools that specializes in bringing together students from many different countries, and Charles believes that these schools can provide many exciting opportunities. For example, during his visit to Venezuela, he suggested to the president that a UWC agricultural school should be started that would search for ways to produce food more cheaply and on a wider scale. As Prince of Wales, Charles has to keep well clear of politics, but as president of the International Council of the UWC he can talk to heads of state on matters of importance and have the chance to get things done.

One Commonwealth country where Charles is always sure to receive a warm welcome is Australia – clearly one of his favourite places. Ever since his schooldays at Timbertop, he has made a point of regularly returning there. He says that his time in Australia opened his eyes more than any other experience.

You are judged there on how people see you and feel about you. There are no assumptions there. In Australia you certainly have to fend for yourself. I was fairly shy when I was younger, but Australia cured me of that.

It was during Charles's first term at Timbertop that he had the opportunity to visit missionary stations in Papua New Guinea with his headmaster and other pupils from the school. On his arrival at the capital, Port Moresby, the Prince found thousands of Papuans and Australians lining the streets and the beaches to welcome him and his friends. The party then went inland and visited the village of Wedau and Dogura Cathedral. Charles attended religious ceremonies, watched local dance exhibitions and received gifts galore. What most impressed him was the profound feeling of Christianity throughout the island.

I would like to mention,' he told people later, 'how fresh and sincere I found the church at Dogura. Everyone was so eager to take part in the services, and the singing was almost deafening. One felt that it might almost be the original church. Where Christianity is new, it must be much easier to enter into the whole spirit of it wholeheartedly, and it is rather wonderful that you can still go somewhere where this strikes you.

When Charles left Timbertop, he went home via Mexico, where he stayed for three days, and Jamaica, where he joined his father and sister at the 1966 Commonwealth Games. In Jamaica it was noticed how Charles had changed during his six months at school in Australia. Gone was the shy, awkward,

hesitant schoolboy. In his place there had emerged a confident, amusing and self-assured young man; a swinger, in fact. The Jamaicans loved him and gave him a new title – Charles, the Prince of Hearts. Wherever he went he was surrounded by young people, all eager to hear his wisecracks. Apart from watching the Games, Prince Charles and Princess Anne shot the swirling rapids of the Rio Grande with their father on bamboo rafts. A raft loaded with drinks, picnic lunch and fresh fruit followed, and the trip ended with a swim and lunch on a beach. Princess Anne celebrated her sixteenth birthday on this Jamaican trip. A specially written calypso was sung claiming that the Princess could:

Charm all men throughout the land
And make Jamaican hearts go like bongo bands.

In 1970, on his way back from a visit to Australia and New Zealand, Charles stopped off in Japan, where he visited the Japanese World Exposition (Expo' 70). The Prince spent twelve hours at the fair grounds, which were swept by rain for most of the time. He became the 1,293,474th visitor to the British pavilion and visited 21 pavilions in all, toured the symbol area and attended a reception for 350 people, half of them young people from the 77 nations represented at the fair.

Charles also paid a visit to the ancient imperial capital of Kyoto. While relaxing after a traditional Japanese lunch that included raw fish, he was asked by a geisha girl if his tour was tiring. Charles said it was – and when the girl asked if he would like a massage, he quickly took off his jacket to accept the offer. He sat cross-legged on a straw mat while the girl massaged his shoulders. When it was all over, he smiled and said, 'Arigato, arigato,' which means thank you.

The following February Prince Charles and Princess Anne spent a two week holiday in Kenya. From the start the Prince made it absolutely clear that he had no desire to spend his time lying on a beach.

My idea of a holiday is to do all the things I can't do when I'm not on holiday. Many people think of a holiday as an occasion on which to lie down, go to sleep and do absolutely nothing. I like going off and being energetic, running around in circles and generally appearing absolutely mad. I like going off somewhere really wild and seeing it before it has lodges built all over it.

Opposite: Charles shares a joke with his guides before setting off on safari

It was Charles and Anne's first trip to Africa. 'I have always longed to come and Kenya seems the most sensible and best place to come. There are masses of game to see here,' he told the ever-present reporters.

Charles certainly got the chance to see and photograph plenty of game. He spent four days on a camel safari in the northern frontier region. The Prince and his companions walked partly by day and partly by moonlight in a region inhabited only by nomadic spear-carrying warrior tribes. The party lived on simple food cooked over an open fire and slept in the open in sleeping bags – there were no tents. Charles was wildly enthusiastic about it all and on his return told the waiting press:

That was something I really enjoyed. It was the best thing I've ever done, or one of the best, the sort of enlightened masochism which I go in for. The fun of it is one could really walk about the bush and come across animals suddenly and watch them. All the people who looked after the camels, and the game scouts, thought I was absolutely mad being in a dried up piece of country instead of sitting in hotels and letting the animals come to me.

Prince Charles on holiday in Kenya with Princess Anne

He said one of the most exciting moments was when he spotted a rhino.

The first rhino seen is always a very exciting thing because they are prehistoric, primeval creatures and this was just sort of standing there churning up the dust. Then it came closer and we were trying to see if we could get it to come closer still or perhaps charge us. But it didn't.

And then the party saw a water buffalo. Said Prince Charles, 'It looked at us for a bit as if to say, "What the hell are you doing here?"'

By the end of this safari Charles had seen elephants, rhinos, buffalo and gazelles – just about everything except lions. A British High Commission official who had been in the safari party said,

The Prince really pulled his weight along with everyone else, and he was a very amusing companion. We had a hilarious time. I don't think I've ever laughed so much on a safari.

And Mr Denis Zaphiro, a divisional game warden, commented, 'He is a very tough young man and he out-walked us all. There was nothing we could do that he couldn't do twice as well.'

The Prince did get a chance to see lions before his holiday ended. He and Princess Anne spent three days in the rolling plains of Kenya's Masai Mara

Above: On a camel safari in Kenya
Opposite: Kenya obviously meets with the Prince's approval

game reserve. The royal brother and sister met the press in rough bush country and Charles, dressed in a khaki safari suit and carrying two ostrich feathers in his bush hat, told how he and Anne had disturbed a lion and his mate dozing in the afternoon sun. The lioness raced away when they approached, but the lion remained to stroll calmly past the field car. Princess Anne had also come across an unusually large herd of 150 elephants and had driven within twenty-five yards of them.

Charles and Anne paid a visit to President Jomo Kenyatta and his wife at their presidential residence about twenty-five miles from Nairobi. They had tea and exchanged presents. Princess Anne was presented with a pair of lion-claw earrings, a brooch mounted in gold, a carved ivory wall lamp, and some dress materials depicting Kenyan wildlife. Prince Charles was given a copper gong inscribed with his arms and mounted with ivory tusks, and a gold-mounted lion-claw tie pin and cuff links. Then the Prince and Princess sat under an awning with the President and his wife, Mama Ngina, to watch the

President Kenyatta couldn't persuade Prince Charles and Princess Anne to join the dancing

colourful male dancers clad in leopard and monkey skins, and the women wearing vivid robes of blue, red and orange, with ostrich feathers in their hair.

President Kenyatta then led the royal pair forward among the rhythmically stamping dancers and, having joined in the dancing himself, paused to ask his royal guests to join in. They smilingly declined.

Children also danced and sang and there were more songs from a purple-gowned choir before Charles and Anne took their leave. 'You all danced magnificently – I couldn't have enjoyed it more,' Prince Charles said as he thanked his hosts.

Before leaving East Africa, the Prince said farewell with a broadcast on the bush radio. He called up nearly one hundred remote stations in the flying doctor network spanning 600,000 square miles, roughly the size of Western Europe. 'I am most impressed by your work. Good luck – and I hope you cure many patients,' he radioed. He also chatted to nurses on a tour of the service's headquarters – two metal roofed huts near Nairobi. All in all the holiday had been a great experience for both Anne and Charles, and they arrived home looking suntanned, relaxed and very fit.

The Queen must surely be the most travelled monarch in history and clearly enjoys it, but her eldest son seems set to outdo her and, in fact, is becoming increasingly active in representing the Queen abroad. On one such occasion he attended the independence celebrations of the Bahamas in July 1973. By now he was a practised hand at presiding over the departure of British colonies, having already represented the Queen when Fiji and the Gilbert and Ellice Islands became independent. He was serving on the frigate *Minerva* at the time and came ashore saying he was delighted to be there 'to escape from the clutches of my senior officers.' He told the crowd bulging Nassau's main square and perched precariously on the roofs of surrounding buildings that his ship had visited several parts of the Bahamas and he had fallen 'hopelessly in love' with it.

It provided me,' he said 'with the opportunity to discover the peace and fascination of life on a Bahamian beach – something I had never experienced before and which gave me great happiness and contentment. That is, until I discovered those proverbial grains of sand wedged between the royal toes. So, you see, I carry a piece of the Bahamas with me now wherever I go.

Charles stayed for five days of independence celebrations and Lynden Pindling, the Prime Minister of the Bahamas, took him round on an almost unending series of official events with a broad smile.

When he spoke to thousands of students and people taking part in a youth rally, Charles urged Bahamian youths 'to build on civilization, not to pull it to pieces to see if anarchy works.'

Obviously enjoying the occasion, Prince Charles receives a garland in Fiji

Rounding up the cattle in Brisbane during one of his many visits to Australia

The most important ability in life is adaptability tempered with tolerance,' the Prince continued. 'There are quite large numbers of people who go through life enslaved to the ideals and prejudices that they formed during their youth. That is not progressive thinking.

Charles received an enthusiastic response from the young crowd and left the Bahamas to farewell cheers from a crowd of thousands and the hoots of cruise liners.

It is a point in Charles's favour that whenever he makes speeches he gains the admiration of his audience, but even more admirable is the fact that he writes his own speeches. 'You know,' says his great-uncle Earl Mountbatten of Burma with obvious pride, 'he's the first Prince of Wales ever to write his own speeches.'

Although Charles admires his great-uncle 'almost more than anybody else,' there was one occasion at least when the Prince declined to be influenced.

I had asked him to speak at the Gandhi Centenary Celebrations,' recounts Lord Mountbatten, 'and since I considered I probably knew rather more than he did, I wrote a speech for him. He read it through and then said, "Would you mind terribly if I don't use this? I'll write my own and then show it to you for your comments."

'Well, I looked at what he had written and I wrote down a list of twelve points. He read them through and then said, "Would you mind terribly if I don't use these either?"

Charles has always liked to speak his mind. On a visit to Australia he told Melbourne students that he didn't like exams, he didn't like single-sex schools, which he considered 'unnatural', and he didn't like swimming in Melbourne's Elwood Beach. It was like swimming in 'diluted sewage'.

Other beaches in Australia met with the Prince's definite approval. When he paid an official visit to that country in 1974 he spent as much time as he possibly could in the sea. At Coolangatta, near Cairns, he watched local beach rescue squads in operation in the risky surf and insisted that officials let him ride in the powerful new rescue craft. True to form, once in the boat, he took over the controls himself and sped across the waves.

During that same trip to Australia and New Zealand Charles took a great interest in sheep shearing activities. When he called at a sheep station near Wellington, New Zealand, he swung into action with a pole and pushed a dozen or so bewildered beasts through a foul-smelling dip.

Later that year Prince Charles was able to fit in a second visit to Australia. The main purpose of this visit was to open the giant Anglo-Australian telescope in northern New South Wales and to open the New South Wales state parliament. He was also able to see some of Australia's most desirable grazing country and meet some of his old friends at Geelong School. On his arrival at Canberra at the start of his eighteen day visit he held a press conference and made it clear that he wished to meet as many people as possible during his stay; 'And this does not exclude eligible young ladies.'

Later he flew to Sydney and addressed a joint session of the New South Wales parliament. After reading a message of congratulations from the Queen, he pointed out that one of the key factors in a stable democracy like Australia was an effective monarchy. He also observed that there was a need for royalty to be free from controversy and sectional interest. 'It is only right, I think, that in company with convicts, lunatics and peers of the realm, I am ineligible to vote.' He then explained, 'This is, of course, exactly as it should be – not necessarily in relation to convicts and lunatics, but in relation to the monarchy.'

He also drew attention to the natural link between British and Australian parliamentary systems and pointed out that these systems had an extraordinary capacity for 'improvisation, evolution and change.'

> This I do believe is the system mankind has so far evolved which comes nearest to ensuring stable government. I also believe that the institution of the monarchy, to which, rightly or wrongly, I belong, and which I represent to the best of my ability, is one of the strongest factors in the continuance of stable government.

The Prince's speech had an enthusiastic reception and next day the press announced that he would

Time to relax in the surf in Perth, Australia

probably be Australia's next Governor General. In fact, at that time it would not have been possible, as Charles still had two years to serve in the Royal Navy, but today the post is still considered a possibility for the Prince, who has loved Australia since the time he spent there as a student.

From New South Wales, Charles flew on to Queensland. He sneaked out for a quiet swim at a beach near Government House, but within ten minutes 2000 people had arrived to watch him – just one of the occupational hazards of being Prince Charles!

He later visited Brisbane's Chermside Hospital, which he renamed Prince Charles Hospital. 'I look forward to returning one day and naming it something else,' he joked. He chatted cheerfully to patients in the children's ward and many young faces were wreathed in smiles by the time he left.

While visiting Tasmania, Prince Charles, quite by chance, met a reporter called Philip Beck, who, it transpired, was his former headmaster's son. 'I remember your father well,' he told Mr Beck. 'He caned me once – no, twice. The hidings were for ragging.'

From Tasmania Charles went to Victoria for a five-day tour of the state. He went to the old gold-mining city of Bendigo, a hundred miles north of Melbourne. Crowds waited to catch a glimpse of the Prince and Charles was quick to remark, 'It looks as though you have emptied out some of the pubs. However, I trust you won't waste good drinking time once I've gone into the town hall.' Later he took the controls of a tram along the main street of Bendigo. An official carefully put an 'L' plate on the front, much to the delight of the spectators.

While in the state, he visited another famous gold-mining city, Ballarat. Here he admitted that he found handshaking and waving the most tiring aspects of touring. 'During my investiture as Prince of Wales,' he explained, 'I met so many people and waved so much that I woke up in the middle of the night, still waving, in bed.' The next day he visited his old school, Geelong. The visit had not originally been on his itinerary, but as he was so near, he couldn't resist popping in.

Before arriving in Australia, Charles had spent four days in Fiji, where he had represented the Queen at centenary celebrations of that country's association with the British crown, and the fourth anniversary of its independence. When he arrived in the capital, Suva, smartly dressed in royal naval whites, he was greeted by thousands of children who had lined the route from the airport to the city centre despite a temperature of over 90 degrees Fahrenheit. He enjoyed himself tremendously in this carefree, friendly country. He took part in many

a colourful ceremony and watched with relish the lively performances given by local communities. At the welcoming ceremony at Suva, the Prince drank a bowl of yaqona (or kava, as it's called elsewhere in Polynesia), which was presented to him by a Fijian chief.

At one function given in his honour by a local chief, Charles found himself sitting next to two pretty girls. After half an hour he noticed that the girls moved and two equally delectable maidens were put in their place. After another half hour they changed places with two other girls – and so it went on throughout the feast. The chief had thoughtfully not wanted the royal bachelor to become bored!

During his stay Charles danced with attractive local women dancers, saw some wonderful scenery, and took the salute at a trooping the colour ceremony as part of the centenary celebrations. He also met some amazing characters, including twelve descendants of those chiefs whose council had ceded Fiji to Queen Victoria a hundred years ago. Prince Charles told them that he would not have been allowed to meet them on the same spot where the Act of Cession had taken place if they had not felt that Britain had fulfilled its obligations in accepting Fiji as a colony, bringing order and tranquility to their war-torn land. He went on to tell the chiefs that Anglo-Fijian friendship had since been based on an almost unique mutual respect and understanding, not greatly changed since the advent of independence. 'The strength of these bonds has no reason, as far as I can see, to wither and disappear,' he said.

A year later Charles was back in the Pacific region, this time to represent the Queen at the independence celebrations of Papua New Guinea. Here he proved himself a great hit by speaking Pidgin English to tribesmen in the Eastern Highlands. At one time he was even invited to judge a village beauty contest, but having watched, with some amusement, two old men prodding and pinching the girls like prospective buyers at a cattle market, he declined the honour as delicately as possible.

In February 1975 Prince Charles represented the Queen at the coronation of the King of Nepal. He was accompanied on this trip by his great-uncle Earl Mountbatten of Burma. On their way to Nepal they paid a brief visit to New Delhi, where the Prince led the Plumed Coronets in a four chukka exhibition polo match against the Ashoka Lions at the Jaipur Polo Ground. The Prince scored two goals, one from eighty yards, and his team beat their opponents by nine goals to six. The Jaipur Polo Ground, where in 1922 the Prince's great-uncle the late Duke of Windsor played as Prince of Wales, seemed to re-echo the lavish days of the Raj.

After being entertained to lunch by the Prime

Minister, Mrs Gandhi, at the President's Palace, Lord Mountbatten showed his great-nephew the rooms of Rashtrapati Bhavan, the palace designed by Lytyens where he lived as Viceroy and, for a short period after independence, as Governor General.

Meanwhile, there was frantic activity in Katmandu. Thousands of workers were completing the preparations for the coronation. Street lamps were being replaced, buildings cleaned and roads improved so that everything would be shipshape for Monday, 24 February, the day determined by the royal astrologers for the coronation. It was also decreed that the ceremony must start at 7 am, which was considered the most auspicious time of day.

King Birendra, who was 29 years old at that time, is the only Etonian king now reigning, and the only monarch who is a Hindu. He is the tenth king of the Shah dynasty. Among the guests invited to his coronation were the Duke of Gloucester, who had been the king's contemporary at Eton, the Duchess of Gloucester and fifteen more of his former schoolmates, as well as his old housemaster.

King Birendra was crowned inside the ancient Hanuman Dhoka, the former residence of the monarchs of Nepal. Before the crowning actually took place, the King underwent a series of cleansing rites. He was smeared with mud from symbolic locations, and then ceremonially cleansed with butter, milk, yoghurt and honey in an hour-long ritual. Cleansed, King Birendra stepped into the courtyard and, accompanied by his queen, Aishworya, mounted the golden throne.

The Royal Astrologer consulted his pocket watch, and, seeing the time was propitious, gave a signal to the high priest. The high priest turned to Birendra to announce, 'For the welfare of the people, I am about to crown you.' And Birendra responded, 'For the welfare of the people, I am ready to be the king. I will be popular like the raindrop, I will be friendly like the sun.' As the magnificent crown set with diamonds, pearls and emeralds, and surmounted with bird of paradise feathers, was placed on the King's head, bugles were sounded and fireworks let off in celebration.

After the ceremonies were over, the King and Queen, riding a richly decorated elephant, went out to be acclaimed by the people. Thirty more elephants followed carrying foreign dignitaries, among them Prince Charles.

The coronation had gone like clockwork. And Charles, looking resplendent in his naval uniform, was a perfect representative of the people of Britain. He impressed not only the people of Nepal, but also Madame Marcos, the wife of the president of the Philippines.

In Katmandu he received a new medal specially struck for the coronation, the star of a Nepalese order, and a mayoral-type chain, the purpose of which is understood only by its donors. Nonetheless, it was gratefully received.

Prince Charles's brief visit to New Delhi on his way to the coronation had proved a great hit and he was invited back for a more comprehensive tour of India. An itinerary was arranged that would give him a glimpse of the many aspects of Indian life. The visit was planned for October, but, much to Charles's disappointment, the trip was later called off at the advice of the Foreign Office. The decision was taken because of the unstable political situation in India at that time; Mrs Gandhi had suspended the normal democratic machinery and placed the country in a state of emergency. There were fears for the Prince's safety because of the risk that his visit might have been used by opposition extremists to embarrass the New Delhi government.

Of course, wherever he goes, both at home and abroad, Prince Charles presents a tremendous security risk. Like the Queen, he considers it an essential

Wherever he goes Charles seems to be greeted by beautiful women. Here he receives a traditional garland as he arrives in Nepal to attend the king's coronation in 1975

Charles in Nepal for King Birendra's coronation. At his side is Mrs Marcos, wife of the president of the Philippines

part of his life to mix with the general public, and more and more he is getting into the royal habit of going on 'walkabouts' among crowds. To add to the security men's dilemma, Charles loves to 'have a go' at things; whether it's jumping from an aeroplane in a parachute or diving beneath the ice, he has certainly risked his neck more often than most.

On trips abroad local police carry out rigid security procedures, but the general public cannot all be screened and there is always the fear that some crank who has a grudge against the royal family will get a chance to make his point. Charles has two regular detectives chosen from the London Metropolitan Police, who take it in turn to protect the Prince and travel with him at all times.

Before each foreign visit that Charles undertakes,

an advance party is sent out to investigate every imaginable detail so that when the Prince arrives everything will run like clockwork. The Prince's medical records are sent ahead and hospitals alerted en route in case of an accident. When the time comes for the Prince to set off, he is accompanied by an efficient team, usually including his private secretary, Squadron Leader David Checketts, an equerry, a press secretary, a secretary to his private secretary, a valet, an air attaché (if he's going by air) and, of course, at least one armed personal detective.

A full set of mourning clothes and black-edged notepaper are carried, just in case a member of the royal family dies while the Prince is away. All in all, about fifty pieces of luggage are needed for the average trip abroad. The Prince needs an enormous variety of clothing, from full-dress uniforms to safari suits, from polo gear to plain grey suits.

Prince Charles is determined to be useful, and firmly believes that one of his major roles could be as an unofficial trade ambassador for Britain. He already does a great job promoting British industry overseas and now realizes the importance of studying industrial relations in Britain so that he can better defend Britain's record overseas. During his visit to the United States in 1977 Charles was determined to prove that Britain still has a lot to offer. In Los Angeles he told a distinguished audience of 1500 people,

> Britain is a modern up-to-date society which is still in the forefront of technological and industrial advance, from nuclear power to Concorde.
>
> 'In the past few years,' he continued, 'it would be true to say Britain has had an unfortunate image overseas, certainly as far as her industrial relations are concerned. We are constantly told that we are going to the dogs and are finished as a nation, by various

Prince Charles on a visit to Bordeaux in 1977 is escorted by M. Jacques Chaban-Delmas

American television commentators. In actual fact, things are not nearly as bad as they are made out to be. In a survey conducted by the International Labour Office in industrial countries, between 1966 and 1975, it was shown that the number of days lost per 1000 workers in Britain was lower than in the United States.

The Prince continued his back-Britain campaign when he visited Brazil and Venezuela some months later. In Brasilia he commented, 'I will do my best to persuade British businessmen that this country has a splendid and exciting future economically and that it is well worth while getting involved.'

In Venezuela he was credited with landing a £1¼ million export order for a British firm. He had visited a Venezuelan gold mine and, just after, it was announced that the British firm, Head Wrightson, had landed the contract to modify the gold ore treatment plant. It was clear that the Prince's visit had speeded

Opposite: Charles meets some of the tribal chiefs in Ghana

things up. 'I hope people's ears were burning in this country when I was travelling around South America,' he said on his return. He told journalists,

'When I go abroad I feel proud to be British.' And he went on to tell them, 'Stop reporting the bad news and start reporting some of the good. The country's morale can be seriously harmed by what the media choose, or don't choose, to emphasize. The British are past masters at self-denigration. Practised reasonably, that's an attractive trait. But sometimes we go too far and are only reminded of the few things that we don't do well. I mean the strikes that occur in a small proportion of our industries, or the unpleasant things that foreigners say about us, rather than the infinitely more frequent complimentary remarks which they make.'

I remember only too well,' he continued, 'somebody telling me not so long ago that, regrettably, it doesn't make news that fifty jumbo jets landed safely at Heathrow Airport yesterday, but it does make news if one doesn't. I still believe, however, in the necessity of reminding people – metaphorically – that vast numbers of jumbo jets do land safely.'

During the Queen's Silver Jubilee year Prince Charles did more than his fair share of travelling,

spreading goodwill wherever he went. In March 1977 Charles went to West Africa, which proved to be among the most colourful and exciting visits he had ever made. He began his trip in Ghana, where he was the first visiting member of the royal family since the Queen made a state visit there in 1961. One of the main purposes of the visit was to attend the fiftieth anniversary celebrations of the Achimoto School in Accra. He also met the President of Ghana, General Acheampong, who proudly gave him a book of his best speeches. He attended the passing out ceremony of military cadets at the Military Academy in Accra, planted a tree in celebration of jubilee year, visited irrigation schemes and even managed to fit in a game of polo in the blazing heat. His team lost 3–2, but he scored both goals!

He was created a chief in a ceremony at the Volta River Dam and eagerly donned a stripped cotton tribal robe for the occasion. Throughout the rest of the tour he was accorded the raised seat and parasol of his status.

Perhaps the most exciting time for the Prince was when he travelled to the north of the country to

Opposite: Charles toasts the Queen during a state banquet given in his honour in Accra, capital of Ghana
Below: The Prince poses in a group picture with proud cadets in Ghana

attend a 'durbar' in his honour. There all the tribal chiefs gathered to greet the representative of Her Majesty in her Silver Jubilee year. It was an incredible sight. The chiefs wore bright robes of every colour under the sun and gold galore. For some of them the weight of all their rings and bangles was just too great, and a boy had to walk in front of them so that they could rest their arms on his shoulder. Charles found he was immensely popular and wherever he went he received a tremendous welcome.

From Ghana the Prince flew to the Ivory Coast for a three-day visit. It was the first major visit by British royalty to French-speaking Africa and Charles was amazed by his welcome. The entire city of Abidjan, which calls itself the Monte Carlo of West Africa, was en fete to greet him. 'I thought

Left: Charles dons the striped cotton robes of a tribal chief. At his feet sits his personal medicine boy
Opposite: Charles arrives in Abidjan, capital of the Ivory Coast, and is amazed by the warmth of his welcome
Below: In soaring temperatures the Prince visits Kamazi, where he meets the Ashanti chiefs. This durbar produced one of the biggest gatherings of the Ashanti tribe, who had turned out in force to welcome Charles

there would be people cheering, but not all those people,' he told members of his party. 'I have never seen anything like it.'

As he drove through the town in a mile-long procession of official cars, the hundreds of thousands of people lining the route shouted 'Vive Grande Bretagne' and 'Vive Prince Charles'. They waved their flags and danced and sang. Women and children were wearing special dresses with a handsome portrait of Prince Charles painted on them and many waved placards with the same picture. On the outskirts of the town the Prince passed under a huge arch decorated with lights saying in French: 'The Town of Abidjan welcomes His Royal Highness the Prince of Wales.'

Charles was the guest of the President of the Ivory Coast, Felix Houphouet-Boigny, and made an immediate hit by replying in French to a speech of welcome by the President. He modestly asked his hosts to be indulgent if he massacred the French language. 'I hope I may have the opportunity to find, perhaps, a brilliant Ivorian female teacher.'

On the second day of his visit the Prince made a short cruise to inspect the harbour installations and, wearing an open-necked, white tropical uniform of a Royal Navy commander, he lunched at the Yacht Club. He also visited the President's plantation estate 150 miles north of Abidjan.

Top: Prince Charles is welcomed to the palace of President Felix Houphouet-Boigny of the Ivory Coast
Above: Charles meets some of his fan-club when he arrives in the Ivory Coast
Opposite: The Prince pleases photographers by posing in naval summer uniform on a beach in the Ivory Coast

The visit was an enormous success and filled the Prince with enthusiasm about the prospects of an expansion of British exports to the Ivory Coast. Thanks to Charles, Britain had gained an important new link with the former French colony.

In July 1977 Prince Charles returned to Canada. It was a tour that added even more to the already great popularity of the heir to the throne in that great Commonwealth country. He spent the five-day visit in Alberta. Having stayed the first night in Calgary, the next morning he flew deep into Indian territory and took part in the re-enactment of the signing of a treaty ceremony that had taken place a hundred years before between the Blackfoot tribes and Queen Victoria. As the Prince pow-wowed with the Indians, they made a protest to him about their treatment by white Canadians. Their leader, Chief Nelson Small Legs, told the Prince,

> It is evident that the trust of our ancestors has been betrayed. Even though the treaty was obviously one-sided in favour of the new-comers, their greed is yet insatiable. They now call our treaty outdated and unworthy of the paper it is written on – the very same treaty which was devised by the Queen's representatives. When our ancestors brought out the pipe of peace they expected to receive fair treatment.

Charles agreed that there were hardships on the Indian reserves and told the Indians that the Canadian government leaders had expressed their determination to find effective solutions to the problems. He moved in and out of tepees, and expressed his interest in the construction of these mobile homes. When the pipe of peace was handed around, the non-smoking Prince did not hesitate to join in. Dressed in tan safari jacket, khaki trousers and pointed cowboy boots, he sat cross-legged on the ground while he listened to long speeches by the chiefs.

The next day Charles was made an honourary chief and given the name Red Crow.

HRH Red Crow was quite a sight as he donned his chieftain's head-dress, buckskins and moccasins, and had his face painted red and yellow by a medicine man. Drums thumped out Indian rhythms and the braves whooped as he joined his hosts in the sacred Sun Dance circle. There he joined in a Grass Dance, Moon Dance and Chicken Dance. It was a scene from a thousand movies, but Prince Charles

Opposite: Formally dressed as Chief Red Crow
Below: The Prince chats with Blackfoot representatives inside a tepee

Opposite: Wearing a traditional Stetson and suit, Charles is surrounded by a bevy of beauties as he watches the famous Calgary rodeo
Right: Looking slightly self-conscious in his Indian headdress, Prince Charles addresses the tribe
Below: Charles agrees to have his face painted when he joins in Indian tribal celebrations
Bottom: Charles takes to a buggy during his visit to Alberta

Riding the cable car in San Francisco

had never starred in one before and obviously enjoyed the fun of it all. Afterwards he was presented with a pinto horse, Indian blankets and saddle, and then it was back to cowboy country for the Prince as he returned to Calgary for the rodeo.

Back in Calgary, Charles was joined by his younger brother, Prince Andrew, who was at school in Canada at that time. 'Howdy, partner,' Charles greeted his brother in true cowboy fashion as he swept a giant Stetson hat off his head.

The two brothers were quick to gain the admiration of the crowds, as they wholeheartedly entered into the spirit of the occasion. Charles led the great Stampede Parade dressed as a cowboy, while Andrew took a front seat in the reviewing stand looking every inch a cowboy in a denim suit and Stetson hat. When Charles passed the reviewing stand at the head of miles of beauty queens, cattle,

cowboys and Indians, Andrew raised his Stetson in a huge exaggerated salute. Then Charles looked down at him from the saddle of his big, black horse and bowed low. The crowds erupted in laughter and later Charles joined his brother in the reviewing stand. Calgary holds the world's greatest rodeo and cowboys come from all over Canada and the United States to take part in the contests. When the royal brothers arrived at a platform by the rodeo arena to watch the various events, they were surrounded by a bevy of beautiful women, all eager to chat to their handsome young heroes. Everyone agreed that the royal heart-throbs were a smash hit!

In October Charles made a twelve-city goodwill tour to the United States and again attracted the attention of scores of eager young ladies. When he spoke at a dinner hosted by the Mayor of Houston, he had the oil tycoons and civic leaders doubled up with laughter by referring to a future 'sex tour' of America. He said that he had revealed to an American girlfriend during the trip: 'I would like to make a sporting tour of America. And she said to me, "Indoors or outdoors?" My reply is not on record.' He then went on to remark about the number of millionaires in Texas. 'I thought about all those daughters,' he continued amid howls of laughter. 'Oil wells are very valuable as dowry.'

In Hollywood Charles attended what was said to be one of the most star-studded dinners in that town's history. Dean Martin entertained the guests as the Prince sat flanked by 'Policewoman' Angie Dickinson and Farah Fawcett-Majors of 'Charlie's Angels' fame.

He's a beaut,' observed Angie. 'I'm blessed that I sat next to him. He doesn't have to be a prince, he's got the charisma anyway. He was wonderful.' And Farah joked, 'Prince Charles should have his own television show – it would be the biggest success on the "heir waves".

Cary Grant made an introductory speech, and when he stumbled over his words, he laughingly remarked, 'It must be my teeth.' When the time came for Charles to reply, he said, 'I'm horrified to speak about matters I know little about. Nerves are overcoming me. Perhaps I can borrow Cary Grant's teeth. They might fit me better than him.'

The evening proved a tremendous success and all the guests were amply entertained by Dean Martin, who joked, 'I sure would like to be a prince and take out a princess. At the end of the evening I'd say, "Your palace or mine?"' Comedian Bob Newhart and a mime act, Shields and Yarnell, also took part in the entertainment. As the evening drew to a close, Charles told his fellow-guests,

It's been an amazingly enjoyable evening. I'm sitting between two of the most beautiful cops I've ever met. I only wish it were possible to arrange a swop with some of my policemen. I've been trying to persuade them to do that for years, but they won't agree.

The following day Charles left for San Francisco, but he promised the stars, 'I want to come back to see you again.' In San Francisco the Prince went to a performance given by the San Francisco Opera Company and afterwards went backstage. One of the performers, Miss Pamela South, told reporters that she had waited for years to tell the Prince that they shared the same birthday, November 14. The Prince told her they should get together next year to celebrate. Miss South said afterwards with a sigh, 'He's so eligible and I'm so eligible.'

After his visit to America, Prince Charles flew on to Australia and again was greeted by pretty girls wherever he went. It was quite a year for the happy young bachelor!!

Early in 1978 Charles made a visit to South America, and, in his usual relaxed manner, charmed his way into the hearts of everyone he met – especially the girls! It was the Prince's first official visit to that part of the world and he did a superb job of promoting the British image. He began the tour in Brazil's colourful sea port, Rio de Janeiro. Here he visited the Brazilian naval installations and harbour, called on the governor, made an investiture, visited factories, laid a wreath to the Brazilian Expeditionary Force and held a press reception – to mention just a few of his activities. But it was a party given by the Mayor of Rio that caused the biggest sensation. A procession and dancing by the winning Samba School caused great merriment, and with everyone wearing fantastic carnival costumes, the whole scene was a joy to watch. The guests at the reception were expected to join in and Charles received tumultuous applause from his fellow guests as, hand in hand with energetic dancers, he joined in a riotous samba. Wearing formal evening clothes, he managed to demonstrate his skills superbly and the following day newspapers all over the world carried pictures of the dancing Prince.

The next stop on Charles's tour was Sao Paulo. Here he had a packed programme, but still managed to fit in a game of polo. With the temperature well into the eighties, he was soaked in sweat by the end of the match, but, as usual, enjoyed the game to the full. He also paid a visit to the Butantan Institute and watched, fascinated, as he was taught about the extraction of cobra venom, which is used as an antidote to snake bites.

In the futuristic Brazilian capital, Brasilia, he met President Geisel and toured the modern public buildings. He also opened the Cultura Inglesa and planted a tree at the Clube Naval.

The Prince visited the Brazilian Agricultural Research Organization the next day, where he toured experimental fields and was photographed eating the kernel of a soybean. When a photographer requested him to eat just one more, Charles was quick to respond, 'Bloody hell.' He was later presented with a gaucho saddle. Wearing a safari jacket and beige slacks, he was anxious to try it out and to the delight of his audience, climbed into it and went on a mock-ride.

Top: Prince Charles emerges from a submarine while visiting naval installations during his visit to Brazil
Above: Walking among the modern buildings of Brasilia, capital of Brazil

Opposite: The Prince receives an enthusiastic welcome when he visits the British School in Rio

Opposite and above: Charles demonstrates his skills as a samba dancer at a party in Rio de Janeiro

Opposite: Charles is delighted with this beautiful gaucho saddle presented to him in Brazil

Above: Charles chats to a group of scouts in São Paulo, Brazil, giving them a day to remember

The Prince on Tour

Prince Charles has travelled widely as an official representative of the Queen, as a naval officer, and as a private person. Below is a list of some of the countries he has visited since 1970.

1970
France
New Zealand
Australia
Japan
Canada
United States
Fiji
Gilbert and Ellice Islands
Bermuda

1971
Kenya

1972
France
Germany
Spain
Holland

1973
Germany
St Kitts
Bahamas
Luxembourg

1974
New Zealand
Fiji
Australia

1975
India
Nepal
Canada
Iceland
Papua New Guinea

1976
Canada

1977
Kenya
Ghana
Ivory Coast
Monaco
France
Canada
United States
Australia

1978
Brazil
Venezuela

During a visit to Fiji Prince Charles was royally entertained to a beautiful display of traditional dancing

During his stay in Brazil the Prince also flew north, deep into Amazon country. At the equatorial jungle city of Manaus he stood by two of the world's mightiest rivers, the Amazon and the Rio Negro. He received an enormous welcome in this city, and hundreds of children turned out to mob him. By boat he visited the floating harbour and customs house of the ancient city.

From Brazil, Charles flew on to Venezuela, where he received an equally enthusiastic welcome. He visited an aluminium plant, tried his hand at bricklaying and paid a call on President Perez. In fact, he packed as much as possible into his time there, including polo. He managed to get in a brief trip to Venezuela's National Park, which was a far cry from the industrial centre of the capital, Caracas. At the National Park he relaxed in what must be among the most beautiful scenery in the world. He made friends with the director's three daughters,

Top: Pursued by press and television photographers, Charles speeds up the Amazon and fades away into the sunset and the retreat of his hotel

Above: It's a dream come true for one young lady as she actually gets to kiss her Prince Charming during his visit to Venezuela

Opposite: The Prince visits an aluminium plant during his visit to Venezuela in March 1978

who joined his boat trip back after his stay there.

Another tour over, Prince Charles could return home safe in the knowledge that the official foreign visit had, as usual, more than paid for itself in goodwill alone and that the future held even brighter prospects.

Family Album

The royal family are a balanced, happy family with a tremendous sense of unity. They love to be together. Prince Charles readily admits that he is happiest when he is with his family and, indeed, the big get-togethers to celebrate Christmas or birthdays must bring a welcome relief from the pressures that normally surround the heir to the throne.

The Prince firmly believes that the family unit is one of the most important aspects of our society and 'ensures to a certain extent an open society rather than a closed one.' He has been accused by some of being a bit old-fashioned in his attitudes, but is quick to retort,

> If being old-fashioned means fostering a good family atmosphere, then I am proud to be old-fashioned and will certainly remain so.

Charles belongs to a very close-knit family and when he travels abroad he keeps in constant touch by telephone or letter. He has both a great respect and a great affection for his parents. In speeches he never refers to the Queen as 'my mother', but always as 'the Queen'. He is, however, more informal with regard to Prince Philip, often calling him 'my father'. It was George V who once said, 'My father was frightened of his father . . . I was frightened of my father . . . and I'm going to see to it that my children are frightened of me.' Luckily, royal paternal attitudes have changed considerably since then and Prince Philip enjoys a very close relationship with all his children, based, not on fear, but on love and respect for each other's achievements.

In some ways Charles seems to take more after his mother than his father. Like the Queen, he is gentle and kind, instinctively shy and immensely conscientious, with a sense of duty always well to the fore. From his father he has inherited his zany sense of humour, and they have particular mannerisms in common, such as the habit of clenching their hands behind their backs and, in conversation, clawing the air with both hands. They also share many sporting interests – polo and shooting for example – experiences, such as their schools and the Royal Navy, and an active concern for the youth movement and the preservation of the environment.

> I wasn't made to follow in my father's footsteps in any sense or in any way,' insists Charles. 'His attitude was very simple: he told me what were the pros and cons of all the possibilities and what he thought was best. Then he left me to decide. I freely subjected myself to what he thought best because I saw how wise he was. By the time I had to be educated, I had perfect confidence in my father's judgment. When children are young, of course, you have to decide for them. I'm talking about the later stage when they are old enough to share in decisions about themselves.

The Queen has always wished her children to be brought up as normally and with as little public attention as possible, but, as Prince Philip once pointed out: 'If you're going to have a monarchy, you have got to have a family, and the family's got to be in the public eye.' And being in the public eye is something Charles has in common with his brothers and sister.

Prince Charles has always had a great affection for his sister, Princess Anne, despite the fact that they have very different personalities. Anne has always been more assertive than her elder brother and

Opposite: Every bit the country gentleman: dressed in traditional tweeds and sporting a smart naval beard, Charles rides the acres of Badminton

Above: Prince Charles with the Queen at Windsor
Opposite above: It's a rare moment when all the members of the royal family are abroad together. Here the family poses for photographers at Bromont in Canada, where they went to watch Princess Anne compete in the Olympic Games
Opposite below: During their stay in Canada, Charles kept a close eye on his youngest brother, Prince Edward

has a strong desire to see things done her way. As a result, she sometimes appears intolerant to others, but she has also gained a reputation for being extremely courageous, and very enthusiastic and conscientious when involved in something that really interests her. She has done a marvellous job as President of the Save the Children Fund and as Patron of the Riding For The Disabled Association, and other charities. It is, of course, in the saddle that she has gained world acclaim. In 1971 she won the Individual European Three-Day Event at Burghley, Lincolnshire and was also voted BBC Sports Personality of the Year at the age of twenty-one. The

Above: The Queen with her three sons at the Montreal Olympics

Opposite: Dressed in style, Prince Charles spends a day at Ascot

highlight of Princess Anne's equestrian career must surely have been when she was selected for the British equestrian team to compete in the 1976 Olympic Games in Montreal.

Prince Charles obviously has tremendous respect for his sister's achievements, just as the Princess appreciates her brother's kind temperament and sound judgement. Over the years they have built up great confidence in each other, seldom taking any major steps without discussing them together first.

Prince Andrew and Prince Edward are considerably younger than Prince Charles and Princess Anne, but in no way has the age difference spoiled the relationship between the two princes and their elder brother and sister, and Charles keeps a watchful and affectionate eye on his two younger brothers. Although there is nearly a twelve year gap between Charles and Andrew, they're great friends. From a very early age Prince Andrew showed signs of growing into the most forthright and extrovert of the royal children, and is often described as 'his father all over again'. Even as a child he merited the same tag his father had had in boyhood – 'sometimes naughty, never nasty' – and the Queen herself has conceded that 'he is not always a little ray of sunshine'. Now a handsome young man, he is more settled and is gradually being introduced to his duties as an adult member of the royal family. With his

immense charm, easy going nature, tremendous sense of fun and film-star good-looks he has already graduated to the role of royal pin-up. When he spent two terms at Lakefield College in Canada on an exchange from Gordonstoun, a group of youngsters roamed around with T-shirts bearing the slogan: 'Randy Andy for King.' He may be second in line to Charles in succession to the throne, but in royal heartthrob stakes the two of them are neck and neck!

It is significant that Andrew's general education and experience are as broad as Charles's, and that his preparation in protocol and statecraft is just as thorough. As second in line to the throne, he must face the fact that there is a possibility that one day he might become King of England. One of the interesting facts of British royal lineage is that of the four monarchs before Elizabeth II, two were not born heirs apparent. Edward VII's eldest son, Prince Albert Victor, Duke of Clarence, died before coming to the throne and his younger brother became George V. And his son, Edward VIII, abdicated before he was actually crowned, so his younger brother, the Queen's father, became George VI, although he was not born to be king.

Prince Edward is the youngest of the Queen's four children and, so far, seems to be the quietest and gentlest, never bothering to compete with the boisterous activities of his brothers and sister.

Prince Charles has always had a soft spot for his youngest brother and whenever Edward is in trouble or wants something, it is invariably Charles to whom he turns for help. Indeed, when the young prince discovered, to his horror, that he was the only member of the royal family unable to go to the Montreal Olympic Games because his school term hadn't ended, he pestered everyone so much that in the end Charles took pity and took him to Montreal himself.

It is almost unheard of that all the key members of the royal family should be abroad together at the same time, and it must have been a nightmare for the security forces. But Princess Anne had been chosen to compete in the Montreal Olympics for Britain and that happens to few enough people, let alone a member of a royal family, so it was not surprising that the Queen, Prince Philip, Prince Charles, Prince Andrew and Prince Edward all felt that they just had to go to Montreal to cheer her on. Unfortunately, the Princess's horse slipped in the mud during the cross-country section of the contest and Anne was thrown heavily to the ground and badly concussed. Typical of her courage, she bravely remounted to finish the course, but the slip had put an end to her hopes of a win, which must have been a considerable disappointment to her.

The Queen Mother once called Charles 'my gentle little boy,' and it's not hard to see that her 'gentle little boy' has a great fondness for his grandmother. He often goes to her for advice and a friendly chat and enjoys sharing his experiences with her. The Queen Mother can see many resemblances between her eldest grandchild and her late husband, King George VI, to whom she was so deeply attached, and a great bond has developed between them.

Obviously, as heir to the throne, there are many things that Prince Charles just cannot do. He can't just walk into a pub when he feels like a drink, or pop into a cafe for beans on toast when he feels like a bite to eat. But, far from being bitter, Charles feels that his home life more than makes up for these minor inconveniences.

When we used to talk at sea, sometimes the sailors asked: "Wouldn't you like to be free?" Free from what? Being free isn't doing what other people like to do, it's doing what you like to do.

'I'm not a rebel by temperament. I don't get a kick out of not doing what is expected of me, or of doing what is not expected of me. I don't feel any urge to react against older people. I've been brought up with older people and I've enjoyed it. On the whole, in my youth, I preferred to be with older people. I've observed my father's wisdom and judgment and appreciated it, benefited from it.

'I've never wanted not to have a home life, to get away from home. I love my home life. We happen to be a very close-knit family. I'm happier at home with the family than anywhere else, so I don't feel in any sense that I'm not free.

Prince Charles is the forty-fourth heir to the throne and can trace his ancestors back to such unlikely figures as Mutamid Ibn Abbad Cadi, King of Seville, whose reign began two years after William the Conqueror's, to George Washington, first President of the United States of America, and, some even say, to Mohammed, the prophet of Islam. But today most people only look back to Queen Victoria.

Below left: The Prince, on his way to plant a tree in Windsor Great Park, finds time to stop and chat
Below right and opposite bottom: At Windsor
Opposite above: Accompanied by his grandmother, Prince Charles attends the Thistle Ceremony in Edinburgh

Victoria had nine children who married into several of the royal houses of Europe. In fact, the British royal family is basically of German descent. The name of the royal house became Windsor in 1917 when Britain was at war with Germany and it was considered unwise to have a royal family with a German name. Both the Queen and Prince Philip have many German relatives as a result of the marriage of Queen Victoria to Prince Albert. The Queen and her husband are both great-great-grandchildren of Queen Victoria, and are distant cousins to one another. In addition, three of Prince Philip's sisters married German princes. It is through his father that Charles keeps in touch with his continental relations, often flying over to spend a few days with one or other of them.

Every now and then the question comes up as to whether the Queen will abdicate in favour of her son. Prince Charles has made it exceedingly clear that he can see no reason why the Queen should ever retire.

I don't think monarchs should retire and be pensioned off, say, at sixty as some professions and businesses stipulate. The nature of being a

monarch is different. Take Queen Victoria. In her eighties she was more loved, more known, more revered in her country than she had ever been before. In other walks of life, too, age may bring accumulations of respect – and possibly wisdom – which are valuable to society.

'Looking at the monarchy as objectively as I can, I'd say retirement at a certain age is not a sensible idea. Some kind of unfitness is a different matter, but you must leave it to the monarch concerned. If you look outside this country, King Gustav of Sweden reigned until he was ninety. I think most people agree that Sweden would have lost something had he retired at sixty.

And, indeed it does seem most unlikely, barring some incapacitating illness, of course, that the Queen will abdicate. Far from being frustrated by the prospect of a long wait before he becomes king, Prince Charles is determined that his long apprenticeship should be as useful and productive as possible. He realizes that attitudes toward the monarchy are rapidly changing. 'I fully recognize,' he says, 'that as people become more radical, there may be periods in the future when there is much less interest in having a monarchy.' But he is determined to defend the monarchy and maintains that:

The function of any monarchy is the human concern which its representatives have for people, especially in what is becoming an increasingly inhuman era – an age of computers, machines, multi-national organizations. This, to my mind, is where the future can be promising.

Above: Prince Philip can no longer play polo, but he must be proud as he presents his son with the winner's trophy
Left: Obviously pleased with his day's sport, Charles drives himself away from the polo ground

Charles feels it is very important to get close to the people he will one day rule and on public occasions does his utmost to please people and make them feel at ease. 'The most important thing for me is to have concern for people, to show it and provide some form of leadership.'

His formal title is His Royal Highness the Prince Charles Philip Arthur George, Prince of Wales and Earl of Chester, Duke of Cornwall and Rothesay, Earl of Carrick and Baron of Renfrew, Lord of the Isles and Great Steward of Scotland, Knight of the Garter. One of Prince Charles's earliest ceremonial functions was his installation as a Knight of the Garter in June 1968 in St George's Chapel, Windsor. The Order of the Garter is one of the most ancient and noble orders of knighthood in the world. In all there are seven orders of knighthood: Garter, Thistle, Bath, St Michael and St George, Victorian Order, British Empire and Bachelor.

Now that he is an adult, there are many traditional ceremonies in which Charles takes part. One such event is Trooping the Colour, which is looked upon as one of the most impressive ceremonies in the royal calendar. Many members of the royal family are always present. Each year the ceremony is held on the sovereign's official birthday, a Saturday early in June. The regiment whose turn it is to troop their colour drill daily for six weeks in prepara-

Above: The Queen and the Prince in front of Windsor Castle
Below: Come rain or shine, the royal family were determined to encourage Princess Anne when she competed in the Montreal Olympics

tion for the day itself when the Queen, escorted by her Household Cavalry, rides out of Buckingham Palace and up the Mall to Horseguards Parade, arriving at 11 o'clock on the dot. The pomp and ceremony of the Trooping is exciting to watch and is extremely popular with Londoners and visitors alike.

The triumphal procession through the streets of London on 7 June 1977 as part of the Queen's Silver Jubilee celebrations was another example of the pomp and pageantry that the people of Britain hold so dear. It was a fairy-tale scene as the Queen and her husband waved to the crowds through the windows of the 216-year-old Golden State Coach, which was being pulled by six white horses. Riding just behind, mounted on a sleek black horse and dressed in the tall bearskin and crimson jacket of a colonel in the Welsh Guards, was Prince Charles. What a perfect escort he made for his monarch, and how the people loved it! Later, Charles was to comment,

It was great fun and, when done well and tastefully, there's nothing more marvellous

Left: Charles, wearing a smart blue blazer, arrives at a polo match
Right: A quick look at the camera
Below: Almost unrecognizable under their huge bearskins, Prince Charles and Prince Philip accompany the Queen during the colourful Trooping the Colour ceremony

Previous page: Charles and Andrew at Calgary

The Prince is quite used to going out to meet the people in Britain and abroad. Wherever he goes, he always delights the crowds

than this sort of thing. Judging by the number of people in the streets, and their enthusiasm, they enjoyed it too. Apart from anything else it was the most wonderful expression of happiness and affection for the Queen.

There are occasions when the royal family have the chance to get away and relax together. Windsor Castle, because of its nearness to London, has become a fairly regular weekend home, though it is probably at its liveliest over Christmas when the entire royal family and the staff join together in the festivities. It is also used as a base during Ascot week, when the Queen invites relatives and race-going friends to a house-party.

After Christmas the family move to Sandringham, where they invite friends to stay, arrange shooting parties and find plenty of time for friendly family chats around log-fires. There is little doubt, however, that Balmoral Castle is the royal family's favourite home. It is the perfect place to relax, with its many acres of heather and woodland. They shoot and fish and live very much the life of Scottish lairds, and wear kilts much of the time. On Sunday mornings all the members of the family join the local people for a service at the tiny Crathie kirk. The royal family usually manage to be at Balmoral from August to October and always make a point of attending the Highland Games, which take place at Braemar.

Prince Charles, in common with the rest of his family, is a country lover at heart. The family love attending horse shows and cross-country events, especially if any family member is actually participating. For many years now they have been cheering on Princess Anne at Badminton Horse Trials, which they attend regularly.

Because of his income from the Duchy of Corn-

wall, Prince Charles does not receive a Civil List payment (which is a public salary). Of the estimated £220,000 that Charles receives from the Duchy each year, he gives half back to the state. This leaves him with about £110,000 tax free. The Prince has gained the reputation of being an exceptionally generous young man and hardly ever ignores a request for help from an organization within the Duchy, not to mention the many donations he makes to charities throughout the world.

With a total area of 130,000 acres, the Duchy makes Charles one of the biggest landowners in Britain. Its interests are spread over Cornwall, Devon, Somerset, Dorset, Gloucestershire and Wiltshire as well as the Isles of Scilly. The Prince owns the famous Oval cricket ground in Kennington and has 850 tenants in that area of South London, not to mention the thousands more elsewhere.

According to those who work for him, Prince Charles is an easy-going and tolerant master. He tries to be a good landlord and treat his tenants fairly. It was his grandfather, George VI, who referred to the royal family as a 'firm'; with Charles in such an influential position, the family firm looks like having a rosy future.

Left: A kilted Prince Charles accompanies the Queen Mother during a visit to the Highland Games at Braemar
Below: The royal family on the balcony at Buckingham Palace following Princess Anne's wedding

Above: The Prince discusses his performance with the Queen

Opposite: Charles was sure of a warm welcome from the people of Monmouth. The schoolchildren were out in force to catch a glimpse of their hero

The Most Eligible Bachelor

'If I got married, I wouldn't be able to do the samba like I did the other night,' joked Prince Charles to reporters during his visit to South America. Joking apart, Charles seems determined to take his time in choosing a wife, for he realizes that the girl of his choice must not only be suitable for him, but also for his family and his country. His bride-to-be will one day be Queen of England, a job few would relish and even fewer would be capable of carrying out.

The Prince takes a serious view of marriage and wants to be absolutely sure before taking this most important step.

> To me, marriage, which may be for fifty years, seems to be one of the biggest and most responsible steps to be taken in one's life. I think it's sad in a way nowadays that some people should feel there is every opportunity to break a marriage off whenever they feel like it. Originally, the whole point of the marriage contract was that it was for life. Marriage isn't only for the two adults who contract the marriage, but it's also for the children of that marriage, to afford them a reasonable degree of security in their upbringing so that they grow up as reasonable and sensible human beings. I think if you feel you can change your mind and try somebody else at the drop of a hat, then that's sad. I think marriage is something you ought to work at. I may easily be proved wrong, but I certainly intend to work at my marriage when the time comes.

But when will the time come? The heir to the British throne is involved in never-ending speculation about which girl he is REALLY in love with. Charles is seen around with lots of pretty girls, but are they just providing a smoke-screen between the public and the 'real thing'?

The Prince has stated that he thinks about the age of thirty is a good time for marriage, 'after one has seen a great deal of life, met a large number of girls, fallen in love now and then, and knows what it's all about.' Now that he's reached that ideal age everyone is on tenterhooks waiting to hear who his bride will be – the national queen-spotting game is well under way. One thing we can be certain of is that whoever Charles chooses will be someone of impeccable background, someone who will be able to face the demanding round of official functions, of endless handshakes and of being stared at wherever she goes. Charles is only too well aware of this.

> You have to remember that when you marry in my position you are going to marry someone who perhaps one day is going to become queen. You have got to choose somebody very carefully, I think, who could fulfil this particular role and it has got to be somebody pretty unusual. The one advantage about marrying a princess, for instance, or somebody from a royal family, is that they do know what happens. The only trouble is that I often feel I would like to marry somebody English. Or perhaps Welsh. Well, British anyway.

Well, princesses are pretty thin on the ground! The choice of blue-blooded consorts is not as great as it was when Queen Victoria married her children to half the thrones in Europe. But there is one princess whom many believe would make the ideal match for the future king. She is Princess Marie-Astrid of Luxembourg, the elder daughter of Grand Duke Jean of Luxembourg and his wife, Princess Josephine Charlotte, sister of King Badouin of Belgium. 'Asty', as she is called, has many advantages. She is a pretty

Opposite above: The Prince on a drive with Davina Sheffield
Opposite below: Charles and Lady Sarah Spencer share a joke during their skiing holiday in Switzerland

girl with flaxen hair and a fresh country face and, very important, has never been involved in any scandal. She was educated in France, where she studied anatomy, biology and psychology before becoming a nurse in a private clinic. Later, she came to England to study English at the Bell School of Languages in Cambridge. Was this significant? Like Charles, she is keen on sport, and enjoys shooting, skiing, riding, swimming, sailing and fishing. Although she prefers to live as normal a life as possible, as the daughter of one of the reigning royal families of Europe, she is used to being in the public eye and has first hand experience of being a 'royal'. Another point in her favour is that both the Queen and Prince Philip seem genuinely fond of her. They made an official visit to Luxembourg in November 1976 and when just eight weeks later the Grand Duke arrived secretly at Sandringham, it seemed to confirm suspicions that something was in the wind. The Grand Duke is staunchly pro-British. He was educated in England, is a former officer in the Irish Guards and served in the British Army during the Second World War. He surely qualifies as the perfect father for a future Queen of England. When Prince Philip recently went to attend the silver wedding celebrations of Grand Duke Jean and his wife, it was considered as 'just another proof of the close links between the two royal families.'

Charles has always been pretty cagey about 'Asty',

Charles likes his girls to share his interests and Lady Sarah finds no difficulty in matching his enthusiasm for polo

saying he hardly knows her. Yet she has said she has met him several times, and when journalists asked her about a possible engagement, she blushed deeply and replied diplomatically, 'It's better not to answer. I prefer not to talk about it.'

Although the match would be very suitable in many ways, there is one, almost unsurmountable problem – religion. Princess Marie-Astrid is a Roman Catholic and, under the 1701 Act of Settlement, no heir to the British throne can marry a Catholic. For such a marriage to take place, this Act would have to be repealed, and this seems unlikely. An alternative is that Marie-Astrid would have to renounce her faith, but the Princess is known to be a very devout Catholic, so this seems out of the question. Talks between Roman Catholic and Church of England representatives are reported to have taken place and one solution to the problem seems to be that, should the marriage take place, the Princess could retain her faith, but any sons of the marriage would become Protestants and the daughters Catholics. This again poses problems: the royal couple may only have daughters. Then, presumably the line of succession would pass on to Prince Andrew.

For a short time there was speculation that Prince

Top: Lady Jane Wellesley accompanies Charles to a
polo match
Left: Charles relaxes at Windsor with Caroline Longman
Right: The Prince with Lady Sarah Spencer at Ascot
Opposite: The Prince talks to Princess Caroline of
Monaco, while Cary Grant looks on

Charles might marry Princess Caroline of Monaco, but this quickly died when he was heard to quip to reporters during a visit to Monte Carlo: 'I have only met the girl once and they are trying to marry us off.' Now, of course, we all know that Princess Caroline has given her heart to Frenchman Philippe Junot and so is no longer in the running.

There is no shortage of other candidates, and many people believe that Charles will marry some-one from the British aristocracy, someone titled and of an old family. Luckily for Charles, there is no shortage of girls in this category. Among the most likely contenders are Lady Jane Wellesley, the only daughter of the Duke of Wellington, Lady Sarah Spencer, daughter of Earl Spencer, and Lady Camilla Fane, daughter of the Earl of Westmorland. These three girls are all considered to be of suitable lineage. Lady Camilla is the least favoured of the three because of her known flirtations with other men, but her parents are great friends of the royal family and Charles seems to enjoy being with her and has escorted her at Ascot.

Lady Sarah Spencer and Prince Charles have been seen together a lot. She has often accompanied the Prince to polo matches and, even more remarked upon, she was the only unmarried woman present when Charles spent a skiing holiday with friends at a chalet in the Swiss Alps. She insists, however, that they are only chums. In an interview with a women's magazine she confided,

> There is no chance of my marrying Prince Charles. He is a fabulous person but I am not in love with him. And I wouldn't marry anyone I didn't love whether he were the dustman or the King of England. If he asked me I would turn him down. Prince Charles is a romantic who falls in love easily. But I can assure you that if there were to be any engagement between Prince Charles and me it would have happened by now.

Without a doubt, the two have formed a very strong friendship. Lady Sarah has been a guest of the royal family at Balmoral and Sandringham, and she has close royal connections – both her grand-mothers were ladies-in-waiting to the Queen Mother. For a time Lady Sarah suffered from anorexia ner-vosa, but she seems to have surmounted this problem

Left: Charles takes his guest, Lady Camilla Fane, to a polo match at Windsor

Top: The Prince with the Countess of Westmoreland
Above: At Ascot with Caroline Longman

and now appears in excellent health. But is she the girl for Charles? Did she mean it when she said she had no intention of marrying him? Or is Charles perhaps using her as a decoy to keep speculation away from the girl of his choice?

Charles has said,

A lot of people, I feel, have a false idea about love. I think it is more than just a romantic idea of falling madly in love with someone and having a love affair for the rest of your life. It's much more than that: it's a very strong friendship. As often as not you have shared interests and ideas in common, plus a great deal of affection. You are very lucky when you find someone who attracts you in the physical as well as the mental sense.

Could the girl who fits in with Charles's requirements be Lady Jane Wellesly? Many people believe she is the most likely girl. Her background is perfect. She knows how to behave in court circles, seems at ease with the royal family, and is intelligent, unpretentious and independent. After leaving school with eleven 'O' levels and two 'A' levels, she took a speedwriting and typing course, then joined a Fleet Street firm to learn about journalism. She now works for the *Radio Times*.

Princess Marie-Astrid of Luxembourg – could she be the one?

Her parents are old friends of the royal family and have been regular guests at Sandringham since before Jane was born. Jane first appeared at Charles's side in 1972 at the Royal Tournament at Earls Court. In 1973 Charles joined her for a holiday at her family home in Spain, and the couple were spotted happily larking about together in the Spanish sunshine, acting just like any young couple in love. Nobody was surprised when Jane was a guest at Sandringham a few months later to see in the New Year and the British public seemed certain that Lady Jane would become Charles's bride. Ten thousand people turned up to watch the couple go to church. The press hounded them relentlessly and seemed determined to marry them off. Jane obviously found the pressure too much to take; her appearances with Charles ended dramatically and it wasn't long before he was seen with other girls at his side.

However, speculation revived when Lady Jane reappeared in 1977. She spent a weekend at Balmoral and faced the public when she joined the royal family at the Braemar Highland Games. The next afternoon she turned out to watch the Prince play polo and the following January she was again a guest at Sandringham. A close friend of the Prince is reported to have said,

Jane was the first girl he fell deeply in love with. I always thought they would marry, but

Charles with the dazzling Farah Fawcett-Majors

120

The Prince seated next to Margaret Trudeau during a visit to Canada

the pressure on them three years ago was so great it ended their romance. Now they are both that much older, and things could just work out for them.

According to friends, Charles was first attracted to Jane because she is not the 'debby' type. She easily gets bored with the society small-talk of other girls. She is warm-hearted and seems to be sensible and restrained in everything she does; in fact, the perfect lady. At the same time she's not stuffy and is fun to be with. Could this slim, dark-haired, attractive young lady be the future Queen of England?

Yet another serious possibility is Caroline Longman, the daughter of Lady Elizabeth and the late Mark Longman, the well-known publisher. After the lesson Charles learned with Lady Jane, it seems unlikely that he will expose the girl he hopes to win to the press. Perhaps it is significant that very little is known about Caroline in spite of the fact that her mother was a bridesmaid to the Queen and, in fact, the Queen is Caroline's godmother. Charles seems to go to great lengths to keep the friendship quiet, although Caroline has accompanied him to Ascot,

watched him play polo and been a guest at Balmoral. She is not titled herself, but her background is right. She is also stunningly attractive and it's not inconceivable that Prince Charles could have fallen for her in a big way.

Of course, not all Prince Charles's dates need be taken too seriously. Like most young bachelors, he thoroughly enjoys the company of pretty girls and has been described as being 'gentle, a good listener, and one of those men who make you feel you are the only woman in the room.' In turn, the girls 'treat him as a man, rather than a prince.' Throughout the 1970s Charles has been linked with one pretty girl after another. In theory there is no objection to the Prince marrying a girl from the Commonwealth or the United States, but it seems unlikely that he would get to know someone suitable from, say, the United States, long enough to consider marriage. Love at first sight, he feels, is probably infatuation rather than love and Charles would have to get to know a girl extremely well before he could contemplate marriage with her. There has, however, been one American girl who, for a time, journalists considered a 'hot tip'.

Laura Jo Watkins, the daughter of an American admiral, first met Charles when his ship, HMS

Jupiter, was in San Diego in the spring of 1974. She was invited aboard for a cocktail party and then acted as the Prince's unofficial hostess at various social functions. This attractive, tanned blonde from California soon made an impression on Charles and, that June, he invited her to London. She watched him make his maiden speech in the House of Lords, but soon found that their relationship was being stifled by pomp and protocol. 'It was another world,' she later told friends, 'fascinating, but unliveable.' She returned to California and speculation died. It was obvious she would never be happy married to the heir to the British throne.

One factor that must surely considerably reduce the field of eligible young ladies in today's 'permissive' society is that there must never be a breath of scandal about the wife of the future King of England. However much he likes a girl, or even loves her, Charles must always bear this in mind. He could, of course, follow in the footsteps of his late great-uncle, the Duke of Windsor, and put love before the throne, but this is highly unlikely. He takes his duties as heir to the throne very seriously and realizes that two abdications in the space of less than half a century cannot do the monarchy any good in the eyes of the public. No one can see Charles abandoning the throne.

A case in point is Fiona Watson, daughter of millionaire landowner Lord Manton. Charles undoubtedly finds her extremely attractive and the couple have been seen together on many occasions. She is far more flamboyant than the Prince's other girlfriends and has even posed as a nude pin-up in *Penthouse* magazine – hardly suitable qualifications for a future queen. She has also lived with another man and is not considered seriously as a contender. But she's fun to be with and, as Charles says, he wants to meet as many girls as possible and know what it's all about before making his final choice. Fiona, aristocratic as she is, will almost certainly be able to teach him a thing or two about life.

Then, of course, there's Davina Sheffield. This vivacious blonde has undoubtedly impressed Prince Charles. She went to Vietnam to help with relief operations, which surely earned his admiration. She has stayed at Balmoral and Windsor and, even more significant, she went privately to Devon with Charles. She is the granddaughter of the first Lord McGowan and baronet Sir Berkeley Sheffield. Her father died some years ago and, more recently, her mother was murdered by burglars at the family home in Oxfordshire. For some time now, very little has been heard of Davina, which again, could be significant. However, many believe that Davina is out of the running due to her former love life. Her ex-boyfriend confessed to the English newspapers that he and Davina had lived together until she met the Prince. Surely the royal family could never allow that.

Some girls might consider Prince Charles to be a great catch. Money would never be a problem, he owns some of the finest land in England, and his future seems assured. Charles already owns his own home, Chevening House, a seventeenth century mansion set in 3500 acres of some of the loveliest countryside in Kent. A wife would certainly complete the picture! However, Charles is sensible enough to realize that he doesn't want someone who accepts him too readily – she probably just wants to be queen. He wants his bride to realize the problems she would have to face being a queen, and marry him anyway out of love and a desire to help and serve him.

And so the speculation continues. One thing is certain: Charles will wait until he is absolutely sure that he has found the right girl. Could it be that he hasn't found her yet?

Diary of Events

14 November 1948	HRH Prince Charles born
15 December 1948	Christened Charles Philip Arthur George
6 February 1952	Created Duke of Cornwall, Duke of Rothesay, Earl of Carrick, and Baron Renfrew on the accession of his mother, Queen Elizabeth II, to the throne
2 June 1953	Attended the Queen's coronation
28 January 1957	Started at his first school, Hill House
September 1957	Started at Cheam preparatory school
26 July 1958	Created Prince of Wales and Earl of Chester
May 1962	Started at Gordonstoun School
January–August 1966	Attended Geelong Grammar School in Melbourne, Australia as an exchange pupil
October 1967	Started at Trinity College, Cambridge
June 1968	Installed as a Knight of the Garter
1 July 1969	Invested by Her Majesty the Queen with the insignia of Prince of Wales and Earl of Chester at Caernarvon Castle
11 February 1970	Took his seat in the House of Lords
March–July 1971	Attended Royal Air Force College, Cranwell and obtained his wings
September 1971	Entered the Royal Navy
13 June 1974	Made his maiden speech in the House of Lords
28 May 1975	Installed as Great Master of the Order of the Bath
9 February 1976	Took over his first naval command, the minehunter *Bronington*
July 1977	Made an honorary chief (Red Crow) of the Blackfoot Indians

The Royal Family

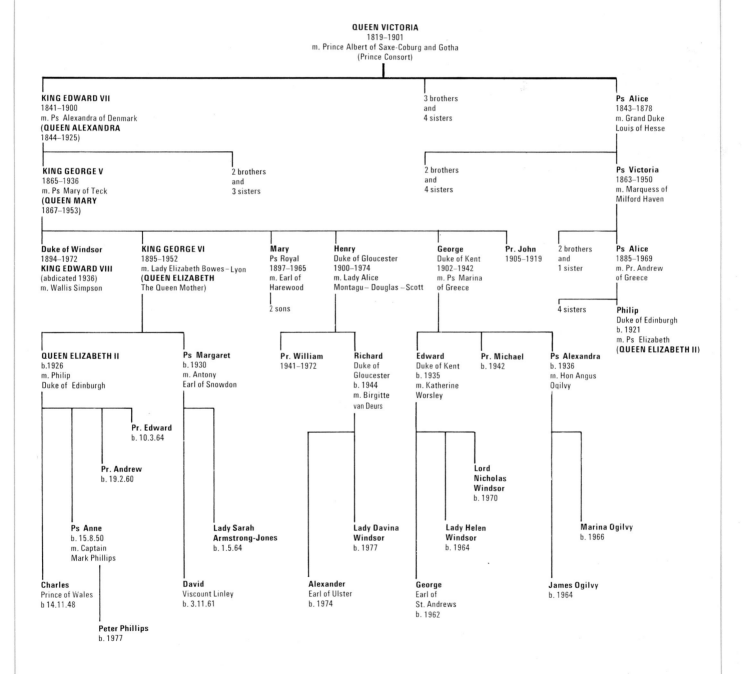

QUEEN VICTORIA
1819–1901
m. Prince Albert of Saxe-Coburg and Gotha
(Prince Consort)

KING EDWARD VII
1841–1900
m. Ps Alexandra of Denmark
(QUEEN ALEXANDRA
1844–1925)

3 brothers
and
4 sisters

Ps Alice
1843–1878
m. Grand Duke
Louis of Hesse

KING GEORGE V
1865–1936
m. Ps Mary of Teck
(QUEEN MARY
1867–1953)

2 brothers
and
3 sisters

2 brothers
and
4 sisters

Ps Victoria
1863–1950
m. Marquess of
Milford Haven

Duke of Windsor
1894–1972
KING EDWARD VIII
(abdicated 1936)
m. Wallis Simpson

KING GEORGE VI
1895–1952
m. Lady Elizabeth Bowes–Lyon
(QUEEN ELIZABETH
The Queen Mother)

Mary
Ps Royal
1897–1965
m. Earl of
Harewood

2 sons

Henry
Duke of Gloucester
1900–1974
m. Lady Alice
Montagu– Douglas –Scott

George
Duke of Kent
1902–1942
m. Ps Marina
of Greece

Pr. John
1905–1919

2 brothers
and
1 sister

Ps Alice
1885–1969
m. Pr. Andrew
of Greece

4 sisters

Philip
Duke of Edinburgh
b. 1921
m. Ps Elizabeth
(QUEEN ELIZABETH II)

QUEEN ELIZABETH II
b.1926
m. Philip
Duke of Edinburgh

Ps Margaret
b.1930
m. Antony
Earl of Snowdon

Pr. William
1941–1972

Richard
Duke of
Gloucester
b. 1944
m. Birgitte
van Deurs

Edward
Duke of Kent
b. 1935
m. Katherine
Worsley

Pr. Michael
b. 1942

Ps Alexandra
b. 1936
m. Hon Angus
Ogilvy

Pr. Edward
b. 10.3.64

Pr. Andrew
b. 19.2.60

**Lord
Nicholas
Windsor**
b. 1970

Ps Anne
b. 15.8.50
m. Captain
Mark Phillips

**Lady Sarah
Armstrong-Jones**
b. 1.5.64

**Lady Davina
Windsor**
b. 1977

**Lady Helen
Windsor**
b. 1964

Marina Ogilvy
b. 1966

Charles
Prince of Wales
b 14.11.48

David
Viscount Linley
b. 3.11.61

Alexander
Earl of Ulster
b. 1974

George
Earl of
St. Andrews
b. 1962

James Ogilvy
b. 1964

Peter Phillips
b. 1977